MONEY, MURDER,
AND THE AMERICAN DREAM

Wilding from Wall Street

to Main Street

by the same author

The Pursuit of Attention:
Power and Individualism in Everyday Life

The Nuclear Seduction:
Why the Arms Race Doesn't Matter—
and What Does
with William A. Schwartz

Power in the Highest Degree:
Professionals and the Rise of a
New Mandarin Order
with William A. Schwartz and Yale Magrass

Professionals as Workers

Money, Murder, and the American Dream

Wilding from Wall Street to Main Street

CHARLES DERBER

Faber and Faber

BOSTON • LONDON

Published in the United States by Faber and Faber, Inc., 50 Cross Street,
Winchester, MA 01890.

Copyright © 1992 by Charles Derber

Library of Congress Cataloging-in-Publication Data

Derber, Charles
Money, murder, and the American dream: wilding from Wall Street
to Main Street / by Charles Derber
Includes bibliographical references.
ISBN 0-571-12917-X: $19.95
1. United States—Moral conditions. 2. United States—Social
conditions—1980–   3. Self-interest. 4. Avarice. 5. Criminal
behavior—United States. 6. Civil society—United States.
I. Title.
HN90.M6D47   1992
306.7′0973—dc20   91-44146
CIP

PRINTED IN THE UNITED STATES OF AMERICA

To Elena

*For rekindling my faith in America
and in myself*

Contents

Acknowledgements

I AM GRATEFUL to many friends and colleagues whose excitement about this book helped it come to fruition. David Karp's enthusiasm at early stages nourished my own belief in the project. Morrie Schwartz also spurred me on with his intuitive affirmation of and insights about the wilding idea. I thank Jonathan Kozol, Howard Zinn, Robert Coles, Philip Slater, and Alvin Poussaint for reading the manuscript and responding to it. I am also grateful to my colleagues Mike Malec and Paul Gray for helpful suggestions, and to S. M. (Mike) Miller for his support and ideas. I am particularly grateful to Noam Chomsky for his corrective insights.

I want to thank Fiona McCrae, my editor at Faber and Faber, for insights that strengthened the work. I also thank Laura Blake, my agent at Curtis Brown.

Ann Cordilia helped me believe that I should take the risk of the new endeavor that this book represented. John Williamson gave me the same encouragement. Ted Sasson demonstrated that students would be excited and challenged by this book. Eunice Doherty's irrepressible enthusiasm convinced me that the book could inform and inspire people in many walks of life.

I owe much to my parents, who nurtured the concern for society that animates this book. And also to Elena Kolesnikova, who heroically endured the obsessions of an author about his work. She contributed ideas, helped me overcome my doubts, and nourished me with those special attentions that kept me off the wilding path.

Permissions

THE AUTHOR IS GRATEFUL to the following publishers and individuals for permission to reprint:

The Boston Globe for quotations from articles from 1989, 1990 and 1991, reprinted courtesy of *The Boston Globe*.

Boston Magazine for passages from the article "Inside the Mind of Charles Stuart," April 1990.

Philippe Bourgois for passages from his article "Just Another Night on Crack Street" in *The New York Times Magazine*, November 12, 1989.

Business Week for a quotation from the article "Warning: The Standard of Living is Slipping," April 20, 1987.

HarperCollins for quotations from *Wealth and Poverty* by George Gilder (1981).

Jossey-Bass Publishers for excerpts from *The Cynical Americans* by Donald Kanter and Philip Mirvis (1989).

The Los Angeles Times for extracts from columns copyright © 1990 by *The Los Angeles Times*. Reprinted by permission.

The New York Times for quotations from articles copyright © 1989, 90/91 by the New York Times Company. Reprinted by permission.

Newsweek Magazine for selections from articles in its 1989 Special Issue on the family.

People Weekly for an excerpt from the article "A Beverly Hills Paradise," March 26, 1990.

The Putnam Publishing Group for excerpts reprinted by permission of the Putnam Publishing Group from *Blind Faith* by Joe McGinness, copyright © 1989 by Joe McGinness.

Random House for passages from *The Hunger for More* by Laurence Shames (1989) and from *The Politics of Rich and Poor* by Kevin Phillips (1990).

Simon & Schuster for excerpts from *The Mountain People* by Colin Turnbull (1987), *The Predator's Ball* by Connie Bruck (1988), and *The Clothes Have No Emperor* by Paul Slansky (1989).

Time Inc. Magazines for excerpts from the article "Catch Us If You Can," March 26, 1990.

The Wall Street Journal for excerpts reprinted by permission of *The Wall Street Journal* © 1991 Dow Jones & Company, Inc. All rights reserved worldwide.

Warner Books, Inc., for passages from *The Circus of Ambition: The Culture of Wealth and Power in the Eighties* by John Taylor (1989).

Woody Allen/PMK Inc. for excerpts from Woody Allen's film script of *Crimes and Misdemeanors*.

Prelude

As I concluded this book with ideas about social change in America, I was reminded of some experiences from my college days. In the 1960s, a few spectators at antiwar marches or rallies would predictably scream, "Love it or leave it." This always struck me as unfair. For one thing, it was an effort to intimidate and silence debate. Moreover, the antiwar protestors often took the risk of getting their heads clubbed precisely because they *did* love their country. One does not bother to criticize that about which one is indifferent. The apathetic citizen, who never votes or protests, might be more legitimately accused of lack of patriotism.

I anticipate that some who read this book will be tempted to respond, "Love it or leave it." I have written a deeply critical essay about America, and many may erroneously conclude that I have no love or hope for my country. But I have written this book only because I am so intensely committed to this society, believe profoundly in its democratic ideals, and do not want to see it betray its exceptional promise.

There is no other country that offers such bountiful material comforts and conveniences, at least for its middle classes. America has no parallel as a consumer society. More important, no country offers quite the same diversity and freedom. For an intellectual, that is an unparalleled gift. And despite the wilding epidemic, the American people remain among the most open, spontaneous, and friendly, and its culture among the most exciting and innovative.

The wilding epidemic looms as a threat that could undermine all these blessings. This book plunges into the infectious core of the epidemic and gives an unsparing portrait of its hazards. Until the last chapter, I do not lead the reader outside the eye of the storm, nor seek to balance its chaos and destruction with the calm and virtue that persist on its periphery. This focus on the most disturbing dimensions of American life is unsettling, but eradicating the epidemic requires the courage to see it in its full proportions.

If this is not a book for those who like to sweep problems beneath the rug, neither is it for those who have given up on America. The dissection of the wilding epidemic in the first six chapters is all preparation for the proposed therapy in the last chapter. The reader may not agree with my remedy, but will have missed my purpose if he or she is not motivated to seek solutions which he or she is equally hopeful about — and equally committed to.

MONEY, MURDER,
AND THE AMERICAN DREAM

Wilding from Wall Street

to Main Street

I

The Good Man
Fills His Own Stomach
All-American Crimes and Misdemeanors

The readings of history and anthropology . . . give
us no reason to believe that societies have built-in self-
preservative systems.

MARGARET MEAD

ON APRIL 19, 1989, in New York City, a group of teenagers ages fourteen to sixteen, went into Central Park.
It was a clear night and not too cold, at least not too cold to
discourage hardy joggers from getting their exercise. The
teenagers dispersed into small bands and began targeting victims for some mischief. One group of six youths came upon
a young woman jogging alone past a grove of sycamore trees.
They cornered her in a gully and began to have some "fun."

That fun would capture headlines around the world. Using
rocks, knives, and a metal pipe, they attacked her. Some
pinned her down, while others beat and raped her. One defendant, Kharey Wise, aged seventeen, told police that he held
the jogger's legs while a friend repeatedly cut her with a knife.
They then smashed her with a rock and punched her face, Wise
said, until she "stopped moving." After half an hour, she had
lost three-quarters of her blood and was unconscious. The
group left her for dead.[1]

What most captured public attention were the spirits of the
assaulters during and after their crime. According to fifteen-
year-old Kevin Richardson, one of the participants, "Everyone
laughed and was leaping around." One youth was quoted by

police as saying, "It was fun . . . something to do." Asked if
they "felt pretty good about what they had done," Richardson
said "Yes." Police reported a sense of "smugness" and "no remorse" among the youths.[2]

From this event, a new word was born: "wilding." According to press reports, it was the term the youths themselves used
to describe their behavior — and it seemed appropriate. The
savagery of the crime, which left the victim brain-damaged and
in a coma for weeks, evoked the image of a predatory lion in
the bush mangling its helpless prey. Equally "wild" was the
blasé mood of the attackers. It had been no big deal, a source
perhaps of temporary gratification and amusement. They were
"mindless marauders seeking a thrill," said Judge Thomas B.
Galligan of Manhattan, who sentenced three of the teenagers
to a maximum term of five to ten years, charging them with
turning Central Park into a "torture chamber." These were
youths who seemed stripped of the emotional veneer of civilized humans, creatures of a wilderness where anything goes.[3]

The story of wilding quickly became tied to the race and
class of the predators and their prey. The youths were black
and from the "inner city," although from stable working families. The victim was white, with degrees from Wellesley and
Yale, a wealthy twenty-eight-year-old investment banker at
Salomon Brothers, one of the great houses of Wall Street.

To white middle-class Americans, wilding symbolized
something real and terrifying about life in the United States
at the turn of the decade. Things were falling apart, at least
in the heart of America's major cities. Most suburbanites did
not feel their own neighborhoods had become wild, but they
could not imagine walking into Central Park at night. Drugs,
crime, and unemployment had made the inner city wild. The
fear of wilding became fear of the Other: those locked outside
of the American Dream. They had not yet invaded the world
most Americans felt part of, but they menaced it. The Central
Park attack made the threat real — and it unleashed fear among
the general population and a backlash of rage among politicans

and other public figures. Mayor Koch called for the death penalty. Donald Trump took out ads in four newspapers, writing "I want to hate these murderers . . . I want them to be afraid." Trump told *Newsweek* that he "had gotten hundreds and hundreds of letters of support."[4]

Six months later, a second remarkably vicious crime grabbed people's attention all over the country. On October 23, 1989, Charles and Carol Stuart left a birthing class at Boston's Brigham and Women's Hospital, walked to their car parked in the adjoining Mission Hill neighborhood, and got in. Within minutes, Carol Stuart, eight months pregnant, was dead, shot point blank in the head. Her husband, a stunned nation would learn from police accounts two months later, was her assassin. He had allegedly killed her to collect hundreds of thousands of dollars in life insurance money and open a restaurant. Opening a restaurant, Americans everywhere learned, had long been Chuck Stuart's American Dream.

White middle Americans instinctively believed Stuart's story when he told police that a black gunman shot him and his wife, leaving Carol Stuart dead and Stuart himself with a severe bullet wound in the abdomen. When Stuart's brother Matthew went to the police to tell them of Chuck's involvement, and Charles Stuart subsequently apparently committed suicide by jumping off the Tobin Bridge into the river bearing his name, some of the threads connecting his crime to the horrible rape in Central Park began to emerge. Stuart had duped a whole nation by playing on the fear of the wild Other. Aware of the vivid images of gangs of black youths rampaging through dark city streets, Stuart brilliantly concocted a story that would resonate with white Americans' deepest anxieties. Dr. Alvin Poussaint, Harvard professor and advisor to Bill Cosby, said, "Stuart had all the ingredients. . . . he gave blacks a killer image and put himself in the role of a model, an ideal Camelot type that white people could identify with."[5]

Chuck Stuart's crime became a national obsession. A twenty-one-year-old Oklahoman visiting Boston told a *Boston*

Globe reporter, "You wouldn't believe the attention this is getting back home. It's all anyone can talk about. I've taken more pictures of this fur shop and Stuart's house than any of the stuff you're supposed to take pictures of in Boston."[6] The quiet Stuart block in Reading had become what the *Globe* called a "macabre mecca," with hundreds of cars, full of the curious and the perplexed, parked or passing by. One reason may have been that white middle Americans everywhere had an uncomfortable sense that, as the decade of the nineties emerged, the Stuart case was telling them something about themselves. Stuart, after all, was living the American Dream and reaping its benefits — a tall, dark, athletic man making over one hundred thousand dollars a year selling fur coats, married to a lovely, adoring wife, and living the good life in suburban Reading complete with swimming pool — a large step upward from his roots in working-class Revere. Had the American Dream itself, by the late 1980s, become the progenitor of a kind of wilding? Was it possible that not only the inner cities of America but its comfortable suburbs were becoming wild places? Could "white wilding" be as serious a problem as the "black wilding" publicized in the mass media? Was, indeed, America at the turn of the decade becoming a "wilding" society?

To answer these questions we have to look far beyond such exceptional events as the Central Park rape or the Stuart murder. We shall see that there are many less extreme forms of wilding, including a wide range of antisocial acts that are neither criminal nor physically violent. Wilding includes the ordinary as well as the extraordinary, may be profit-oriented or pleasure-seeking, and can infect corporations and governments as well as individuals of every race, class, and gender.

The Mountain People: A Wilding Culture

Between 1964 and 1967, anthropologist Colin Turnbull lived among the people of Uganda known as the Ik, an unfortunate people expelled by an uncaring government from their traditional hunting lands to extremely barren mountainous areas. In 1972, Turnbull published a haunting book about his experiences which left no doubt that a whole society can embrace "wilding" as a way of life.[7]

When Turnbull first came to the Ik, he met Atum, a sprightly, little old barefoot man with a sweet smile, who helped guide Turnbull to remote Ik villages. Atum warned Turnbull right away that everyone would ask for food. While many would indeed be hungry, he said, most could fend for themselves, and their pleas should not be trusted; Turnbull, Atum stressed, should on no account give them anything. But before he left that day, Atum mentioned that his own wife was severely ill and desperately needed food and medicine. On reaching his village, Atum told Turnbull his wife was too sick to come out. Later, Turnbull heard exchanges between Atum and his sick wife, and moans of her suffering. The moans were wrenching, and when Atum pleaded for help, Turnbull gave him food and some aspirin.

Some weeks later, Atum had stepped up his requests for food and medicine, saying his wife was getting sicker. Turnbull was now seriously concerned, urging Atum to get her to a hospital. Atum refused, saying "she wasn't *that* sick." Shortly thereafter, Atum's brother-in-law came to Turnbull and told him that Atum was selling the medicine that Turnbull had been giving him for his wife. Turnbull, not terribly surprised, said that "that was too bad for his wife." Whereupon the brother-in-law, enjoying the joke enormously, told him that Atum's wife "had been dead for weeks," and that Atum had buried her inside the compound so you wouldn't know." No wonder Atum had not wanted his wife to go to the hospital, Turnbull thought to himself: "She was worth far more to him dead than alive."[8]

Startling to Turnbull was not only the immense glee the brother-in-law seemed to take in the "joke" inflicted on his dying sister, but the utter lack of embarrassment shown by Atum when confronted with his lie. Atum shrugged it off, showing no remorse whatsoever, saying he had simply forgotten to tell Turnbull. That his little business enterprise may have led to his wife's death was the last thing on Atum's mind. This was one of the first of many events that made Turnbull wonder whether there was any limit to what an Ik would do to get food and money.

Some time later, Turnbull came across Lomeja, an Ik man he had met much earlier. Lomeja had been shot during an attack by neighboring tribesmen and was lying in a pool of his own blood, apparently dying from two bullet wounds in the stomach. Still alive and conscious, Lomeja looked up at Turnbull and asked for some tea. Shaken, Turnbull returned to his Land Rover and filled a big, new yellow enamel mug. When he returned, Lomeja's wife was bending over her husband. She was trying to "fold him up" in the dead position although he was not yet dead, and started shrieking at Turnbull to leave Lomeja alone because he was already dead. Lomeja found the strength to resist his wife's premature efforts to bury him and was trying to push her aside. Turnbull managed to get the cup of tea to Lomeja, who was still strong enough to reach out for it and sip it. Suddenly Turnbull heard a loud giggle and saw Lomeja's sister, Kimat. Attracted by all the yelling, she had "seen that lovely new, bright yellow enamel mug of hot, sweet tea, had snatched it from her brother's face and made off with it, proud and joyful. She not only had the tea, she also had the mug. She drank as she ran, laughing and delighted at herself."[9]

Turnbull came to describe the Ik as "the loveless people." Each Ik valued only his or her own survival—and regarded everyone else as a competitor for food. Ik life had become a grim process of trying to find enough food to stay alive each day. The hunt consumed all of their resources, leaving virtually no reserve for feelings of any kind, nor for any moral scruples that might interfere with filling their stomachs. As Margaret Mead wrote, the Ik had become "a people who have become monstrous beyond belief." The scientist Ashley Montagu wrote that the Ik are "a people who are dying because they have abandoned their own humanity."

Ik families elevated wilding to a high art. Turnbull met Adupa, a young girl of perhaps six, who was so malnourished that her stomach was grossly distended and her legs and arms spindly. Her parents had decided she had become a liability and threw her out of their hut. Since she was too weak now to go out on long scavenging ventures, as did the other children, she would wander as far as her strength would allow, pick up scraps of bone or half-eaten berries, and then come back to her parents' place, waiting to be brought back in. Days later, her parents, tiring of her crying, finally brought her in and promised to feed her. Adupa was happy and stopped crying. The parents went out and "closed the asak behind them, so tight that weak little Adupa could never have moved it if she had tried."[10] Adupa waited for them to come back with the food they had promised. But they did not return until a whole week had passed, when they knew Adupa would be dead. Adupa's parents took her rotting remains, Turnbull writes, and threw them out, "as one does the riper garbage, a good distance away."[11] There was no burial — and no tears.

Both morality and personality among the Ik were dedicated to the single all-consuming passion for self-preservation. There was simply "not room in the life of these people," Turnbull observes dryly, "for such luxuries as family and sentiment and love." Nor for any morality beyond "marangik," the new Ik concept of goodness, which means filling one's own stomach.

America as a Wilding Society

Long before the rape in Central Park or the Stuart murder, Ashley Montagu, commenting on Turnbull's work, wrote that "the parallel with our own society is deadly." In 1972, when Turnbull published his book, wilding had not become part of the American vocabulary, nor did Americans yet face declining living standards, let alone the starvation of the Iks. Americans were obviously not killing their parents or children for money, but they dedicated themselves to self-interested pursuits with a passion not unlike that of the Ik. In America, a land of plenty, there was the luxury of a rhetoric of morality and feelings of empathy and love. But was not the American Dream a paean to individualistic enterprise, and could not such enterprise be conceived in some of the same unsentimental metaphors used by Turnbull about the Ik: The Ik community "reveals itself for what it is, a conglomeration of individuals of all ages, each going his own way in search of food and water, like a plague of locusts spread over the land."[12]

In what may be the most penetrating film on American life as the 1990s dawned, Woody Allen's *Crimes and Misdemeanors* hints that wilding is becoming part and parcel of the American Dream. The movie's protagonist is Judah, a doctor who has it all. A brilliant ophthalmologist, Judah is at the top of his profession and married to a beautiful and loving wife. He has a six-figure income, a gorgeous house on four acres, and is a pillar of the community, known for his philanthropic works. He is cultured as well as rich. "You can call Judah to find out which is the best restaurant in Paris or in Athens, or the best hotel in Moscow, or the best recording of a particular Mozart symphony," says a community leader toasting Judah. Judah is living the American Dream.

Judah's affair with his mistress Delores exposes the shadowy side of the modern American success story. When Delores learns that Judah is not serious about leaving his marriage, she threatens to tell his wife about the affair and to reveal to the world that Judah has dipped into his philanthropy trusts to cover his own cash-flow problems. Judah believes his life is about to go up in smoke. At his wit's end, he calls his brother, Jack, the black sheep of the family who has shady friends from the underworld. Jack assures Judah that Delores can be "handled." "We're talking about a human being," Judah haltingly protests. "She's not an insect. You can't just step on her." He says, "I can't do it. I can't think that way." But shortly thereafter, Judah calls Jack back and tells him to go ahead. Judah pays for the murder and his brother sees that it is carried out. Judah, a man who exemplifies success in the late 1980s, has become a killer.

For a while, Judah is "plagued by deep-seated guilt" and because of his religious upbringing is tortured by the notion that he "has violated God's order." But after many sleepless nights, one morning he "wakes up, the sun is shining, his family is around him," and "the guilt has lifted." Yes, "every once in a while," he has a "twinge" of conscience, but "with time it all fades." Judah accepts that in the real world, we must all "rationalize" and "deny," to live with inevitable moral compromises. The important thing now is that "he is scot free," that "he is not punished," indeed, "he prospers." He can, with a quiet conscience, put this behind him and go back to his life. The difference between Judah, who symbolizes the American Dream, and Jack, representing its dirty underside, has blurred. The viewer leaves wondering whether Judah or Jack is the greater wilder, which leads inexorably to the larger question of what has happened to the American Dream at the end of the twentieth century?

A spate of books about the Reagan era suggest a corruption of the American Dream in our time.[13] Most Americans do not become killers to make it up the ladder or hold on to what they have, but the traditional restraints on naked self-aggrandizement seem weaker—and the insatiability greater. Donald Trump is only the most visible of the American heroes defining life as "The Art of the Deal," the title of Trump's best-selling autobiography. Trump feels no moral contradiction about building the most luxurious condos in history in a city teeming with homeless. Trump writes triumphantly about the Trump Tower in Manhattan: "We positioned ourselves as the only place for a certain kind of very wealthy person to live—the hottest ticket in town. We were selling fantasy."[14] Trump is a living advertisement for Ronald Reagan's manifesto in his in-

augural address, "We are too great a nation to limit ourselves
to small dreams."

In 1835, Alexis de Tocqueville wrote that in America "no natural boundary seems to be set to the efforts of man." But in the
1980s, John Taylor writes, a new version of the American
Dream emerged, both more expansive and more morally perverted than its predecessors. America entered a new Gilded
Age, where the celebration and "lure of wealth has overpowered conventional restraints."[15] Laurence Shames writes that
the name of the American game has become simply *more*.[16]

In the 1980s, yuppies, with their "vaunting ambition and
outsized expectations," came to symbolize this new chapter of
the American Dream. Youthful commodity traders fresh out
of business school engaged in feeding frenzies in the exchanges,
pursuing quick fortunes "as if they'd invented the habit of
more, when in fact they'd only inherited it the way a fetus picks
up an addiction in the womb. The craving was there in the national bloodstream."[17] Many of these young entrepreneurs
would turn to inside trading—and more serious crime—when
their risky ventures went bad. The notorious Billionaire Boys'
Club, made famous in the movie *Wall Street*, would show that
respectable young men consumed by the dream could become
killers.

Shames notes there has always been a tenuous connection
between the American Dream and civilized behavior: "Grabs
at personal prosperity" can "come precisely at the expense of
those civilized and civilizing privileges" that prosperity is for.[18]
The peculiar feature of the dream emerging in the 1980s was
its insatiability, each success and gorging creating a more acute
sense of starvation. Such inability to satisfy chronic gnawing
hunger is fertile breeding ground for a culture of wilding.

The new outsized dream could engulf the entire personality.
The horrifying combination of narcissism and sociopathy, so
marked among the Ik, became the focal point of discussion
among psychologists speculating about Charles Stuart. In the
1970s, culture watchers like Christopher Lasch had already

identified narcissism (a distorted love of self masking inner self-contempt and emptiness) as a mushrooming psychic cancer, the most widespread personality disorder in late twentieth-century America. In the Reagan-Bush era, narcissism became mixed with a deadly brew of sociopathic indifference, cloaked as a virtue in the official rhetoric of entrepreneurship, individual initiative, and self-reliance. The psychological and ideological preconditions of a wilding society were beginning to converge: tortured personalities driven by pounding needs for attention, power, and status in a holy "money culture" embracing the unrestrained pursuit of wealth and self-aggrandizement. Me, Me, Me, hollered the relentless voices from inside; look after Number One, echoed the reassuring voices from high places. The new operational credo: Anything Goes.

For the rich, the unscrupulous, and the driven, the tax and deregulation policies of Reaganomics opened up unimaginable bonanzas. Michael Milken, the "junk-bond king" of Wall Street, demonstrated how literally billions of dollars could be created and pocketed overnight. Such overwhelming enticements proved addicting to a whole generation of business graduates. Everyone could now win the lottery.

As the sociologist Émile Durkheim observed, if the ceiling on ordinary expectations is removed, the conventional restraints on pursuing them will also rapidly disappear. This produces wilding based on unlimited opportunity. Ironically, it resembles the Ik form of wilding, for unlimited opportunity creates not only grandiosity but its own form of starvation. Milken, a man of endless resources, seemed never able to satisfy a hunger bred within and without. Neither could Charles Stuart, a working-class boy making well over a hundred thousand a year when he allegedly executed his wife.

For many other Americans, the economic horizons were closing, not opening. The flamboyant wealth of the Reagan era disguised the steady decline in America's fortunes: the precipitous decline in the American manufacturer's capacity to compete globally, the burgeoning trade deficit, astronomical

public and private debt, and a crumbling infrastructure undermining the prospects for revitalization. To most Americans,
this translated into harder work and harder times. For middle
Americans, it meant never quite keeping up and longer hours;
both husband and wife moonlighting, and still not having quite
enough for the mortgage, the property tax, the utility bill. For
Americans at the bottom, it meant no housing, no medical
care, no job, no education, no money.

For these Americans, in the middle and at the bottom, the
new "gilded" dream became a recipe for wilding based on collapsed possibilities. A dream of *more* has been sustainable when
the pie is growing, as it has been through most of American
history. But when real income begins to decline, an outsized
dream becomes illusion, inconsistent with the reality of most
Americans' lives. Outsized dream, downsized lives. Sociologist Robert Merton wrote that crime is a product of a disparity
between goals and means. To weave grandiose materialist
dreams in an era of restricted opportunities is the ultimate recipe for social wilding.

A new age of limits and polarization in the 1990s sets the
stage for an advanced wilding crisis. In an America more deeply divided by class, the American Dream, and especially the
new gilded dream, can not be a common enterprise and is
transformed into multiple wilding agendas, unleashing wilding among people at every station but in different ways.
Among those at the bottom, the dream becomes pure illusion;
wilding, whether dealing drugs or grabbing handbags,
mushrooms as a survival option and as a fast track out of the
ghetto into the high life. Among the insecure and slipping great
American middle class, wilding becomes a "growth area" for
those endowed with classic American initiative and ingenuity
and unwilling to go down with their closing factories and
shrinking industries. For the professional and business classes
at the top, wilding is sanctified as professional ambition and
proliferates as one or another variant of dedicated and untrammeled careerism. Ensconced inside heavily fortified suburban

or gentrified enclaves, these elite groups also pioneer new forms of social wilding in what Harvard professor Robert Reich calls a "politics of secession": abandoning society itself as part of a panicky defense against the threat from the huge covetous majority left behind.[19] The wilding crisis, as we shall see, arises partly out of a virulent new class politics.

Are We All Wilders? Individualism and the Wilding Epidemic

America now faces a wilding epidemic that is eating at the country's social foundation and could rot it. The American case is much less advanced than the Ik's, but the disease is deeply rooted and is spreading through the political leadership, the business community, and the general population. Strong medicine can turn the situation around, but failure to act now could be irreversible.

Only a handful of Americans are "ultimate wilders" like Charles Stuart. Such killers are noteworthy mainly because they may help wake us to the spread of the wilding plague among thousands of less extreme wilders who are not killers. Wilding includes a vast spectrum of self-centered and self-aggrandizing behavior that harms others. A wilding epidemic tears at the social fabric and threatens to unravel society itself, ultimately reflecting the erosion of the moral order and the withdrawal of feelings and commitments from others to "number one."

The wilding virus comes in radically different strains. There is "expressive wilding": wilding for the sheer pleasure of indulging one's own destructive impulses, the kind found among the Central Park kids or the growing number of American youth who heave rocks off highway bridges in the hope of smashing the windshields of unknown drivers passing innocently below. Expressive wilding can be distinguished from "instrumental wilding": wilding for money, career advancement, or other acquisitive ends, exemplified by Michael Milken and Charles Stuart. Expressive and instrumental wilding have in common a destructive self-orientation made possible by a stunning collapse of moral restraints and a chilling lack of feeling for others. I am mainly concerned in this book with instrumental wilding, because it is the form most intimately connected with the American Dream and least understood in its poisonous effects on society.[20]

While much wilding is criminal, there is a vast spectrum of perfectly legal wilding, exemplified by the careerist who indifferently betrays or steps on colleagues to advance up the ladder. There are forms of wilding, like lying or cheating, that are officially discouraged, but others, like the frantic and single-minded pursuit of wealth, are cultivated by some of the country's leading corporations and financial institutions. Likewise, there are important differences in the severity of the disease. Killing a spouse for money is obviously far more brutal than stealing a wallet or cheating on an exam. But there are distinct types and degrees of infection in any affliction, ranging from terminal cases like Stuart to "intermediate" cases like the Savings and Loan crooks, to those who are either "petty wilders" or who rarely exhibit symptoms at all. The last mentioned include large numbers of Americans who may struggle internally with their wilding impulses but remain healthy enough to restrain them. The variation is much as in heart disease; those with only partial clogging of their arteries and no symptoms are, indeed, different from those with full-blown, advanced arteriosclerosis, and those least afflicted may never develop the terminal stage of the illness. But the differences are normally of degree rather than kind, and the same underlying pathology—whether embryonic or full-blown—is at work among people with mild or severe cases.

There are, nonetheless, real differences between minor "white lies" or small misdemeanors (forms of petty wilding) and serious wilding of the Central Park or Stuart variety. Petty wilding occurs in all cultures, will persist as long as most people are not saints, and in limited doses does not necessarily threaten civil order. When so limited as not to constitute a grave social danger, it might better be described as "incipient wilding" and is not of concern here.

But certain types of petty wilding are growing at an alarming rate in America, as I document in Chapter 5 in my discussion of minor lying, cheating and "ordinary" competitiveness and indifference to others. Such transgressions in epidemic form can reach a critical mass and become as serious a threat to society as violent crime or huge economic scandals like the Savings and Loan crisis. It is not the degree of brutality or violence but the consequences for society that ultimately matter, and we thus consider the full spectrum of wilding acts — both petty and outrageous — that together now constitute a clear and present danger to America's social fabric.

Wilding, sociologically conceived, thus extends far beyond random violence by youth gangs, the current definition of the word offered by Webster's dictionary, to include three types of assault on society. "Economic wilding" is the morally uninhibited pursuit of money by individuals or businesses at the expense of others. "Political wilding" is the abuse of political office to benefit oneself or one's own social class, or the wielding of political authority to inflict morally unacceptable suffering on citizens at home or abroad. "Social wilding" ranges from personal or family acts of violence, such as child abuse, to collective forms of selfishness that weaken society, such as affluent suburbs turning their backs on bleeding central cities.

Economic wilders such as Donald Trump or Leona Helmsley, described as the "Queen of Mean," wife of the hotel mogul convicted of tax fraud, are a different species from the kids in Central Park. Partly because of differing opportunities and incentives, people wild in different ways and for exceedingly varied reasons and motives, ranging from greed and lust to getting attention or respect. The different forms of wilding, however, are all manifestations of degraded American individualism.

Wilding is individualism run amuck, and the wilding epidemic is the face of America's individualistic culture in an advanced state of disrepair. Individualistic culture promotes the freedom of the individual and in its healthy form nurtures human development and individual rights. In its degraded form, it becomes a license for unrestrained and sociopathic self-interest. Individualism — and its excesses — has a different face in the economy in politics, and in the family. The deregulated "free market" created in the 1980s established the environment for the extreme economic individualism that spawned such wilding calamities as the Savings and Loan crisis. Degraded individualism in politics is reflected in the explosion of government corruption detailed in Chapter 3, including the spectacular looting of the Department of Housing and Urban Development and the Department of Defense over the past decade. The manifestations of degraded individualism in families range from casual divorce to emotional neglect of children.

Although the epidemic now infects almost every major American institution, cooperative behavior survives, and in every community one will find idealists, altruists, and a majority of citizens seeking to live lives guided by moral principles. In 1990, seven out of every ten Americans gave money to charity and five out of ten rolled up their sleeves and volunteered or became social activists; these are among the many hopeful indications, as discussed in Chapter 7, that America can still purge itself of this epidemic.

For an analyst of wilding, there are *two* Americas: the America already seriously infected, which is my main subject in this book, and the America that has not yet succumbed and remains what I call in the last chapter a civil society. The majority of ordinary Americans, it should be stressed, are part of the second America, and retain emotional sensibilities and a moral compass that inhibit severe wilding behavior. But, as the epidemic continues to spread, individual interests increasingly override common purposes, and the self, rather than family or community, increasingly grabs center stage in both

Americas. Not everyone will become a wilder, but nobody will be untouched by wilding culture.[21]

Wilders who catch the fever and play by the new rules profoundly infect their own vulnerable communities, families, and workplaces. One dangerous criminal on a block can make his community wild, inducing aggression, violence, and a fortress mentality among peaceable neighbors. A particularly competitive salesman or account executive can turn the whole office into a jungle, since those who do not follow suit and sharpen their own swords may be left sundered in the dust. The new ethos rewards the wilder and penalizes those clinging to civil behavior. One defense against wilding in modern America is to embrace it, spreading wilding behavior among people less characterologically disposed to be wilders and still struggling against wilding as a way of life.

Many Americans misread the epidemiology of AIDS as a problem of deviant and disadvantaged groups. They are at risk of making the same miscalculation about the wilding epidemic, to which no sector of the society has any immunity. Its ravages may be most eye-catching among the poor and downtrodden, but the virus afflicts the respected and the comfortable just as much: the genteel suburbs as well as the inner cities. Indeed, American wilding is, to a surprising degree, an affliction of the successful, in that it is the rich and powerful who have written the wilding rules and it is ever more difficult to climb the ladder without internalizing them.

The progress of the wilding epidemic is shaped less by the percentage of sociopaths than by the sociopathy of its elites and the rules of the success game they help to define. A wilding society is one where wilding is a route to the top, and where legitimate success becomes difficult to distinguish from the art of wilding within—or even outside of—the law.

The wilding epidemic is now seeping into America mainly from the top. While the majority of business and political leaders remain honest, a large and influential minority during the Reagan-Bush era are not only serving as egregious role models but rewriting the rules of the American success game in their own interest. Michael Milken was convicted of massive financial fraud, but his more important contribution to the wilding epidemic was helping change the rules of the American financial game. Similarly, presidents Reagan and Bush have helped invigorate new and morally disturbing codes of conduct, on Wall Street and Main Street, partly by the personal example of figures high up in their administrations, but mainly through the radicalism of their "free market" revolution. As conservative analyst Kevin Phillips writes, Reagan-Bush policy has advanced the most ambitious class agenda of the rich in over a century, an innovative brew of market deregulation and individualistic ideology that, as I show in Chapters 3 and 4, has fanned the flames of wilding across the land.[22]

Neither Presidents Reagan nor Bush, however, invented wilding, nor did they create the individualistic economy and culture that are the long-term and deep-seated breeding grounds of the wilding ethos. The seeds of America's wilding plague were planted long before the current era. A century ago, Tocqueville observed that conditions in America led every "member of the community to be wrapped up in himself" and worried that "personal interest will become more than ever the principal, if not the sole spring" of American behavior. Selfish and mean-spirited people can be found in every culture and every phase of history, and wilding, as we show in the next chapter, is certainly not a new phenomenon in American life. One of the world's most individualistic societies, America has long struggled to cope with high levels of violence, greed, political corruption, and other wilding outcroppings.

Over the last hundred years, American history can be read as a succession of wilding periods, alternating with eras of civility. The Robber Baron era, an age of spectacular economic and political wilding, was followed by the Progressive Era, in which moral forces reasserted themselves. The individualistic license of the 1920s, another era of economic and political wilding symbolized by the Teapot Dome scandal, yielded to the New Deal era, when America responded to the Great Depression with remarkable moral and community spirit. The moral idealism of a new generation of youth in the 1960s was followed by the explosion of political, economic, and social wilding in the current era.

What distinguishes the current epidemic are the subtle legitimation of wilding as it becomes part of the official religion in Washington, the severity of the wilding crisis in banking and commerce, its spread into universities and other vital cultural centers, and the subsequent penetration of wilding culture so deeply into the lives of the general population that society itself is now at risk. As apparent among the Ik, the ultimate casualty of the wilding epidemic is civil society, and the end stage is social ungluing. America has witnessed its share of individual wilders, but never before has the epidemic advanced so far that it threatens to dismantle the family and other vital institutions while also undermining the possibilities of civil order in the greatest American cities.

The wilding epidemic, of course, is not the only cause of the problems in America's schools, families, and cities; moreover, the wilding crisis is as much the result of these problems as their cause. Wilding and institutional unraveling feed poisonously on one another. Thus, as neighborhoods and families erode, partly under the weight of extreme economic burdens, a new generation of wilding kids who lack the security to care about anyone but themselves disrupt schools and workplaces and create even more unstable families of their own. Wilders weaken economic institutions and communities, and the weakened economy and social structure in turn produces new wilding. The spiral is vicious and self-perpetuating.

While perched at a perilous turning point, America has not yet surrendered. Tocqueville recognized a kinder and gentler side of Americans, who were more tolerant, egalitarian, and democratic than Europeans, and who had created thousands of grass-roots organizations to bring Americans together and help them "constantly feel their mutual dependence on each other." These still survive in America as part of a social "immune system," now weakened but still capable of defeating the virus. But to stop and root out the epidemic requires a vision and a passion for change that can arise only by coming fully to terms with the wilding specter that haunts us.

2

The Ultimate Wilders
Rob Marshall and the Menendez Brothers — Prisoners of the American Dream

Why should we be in such desperate haste to succeed?
And in such desperate enterprises?

THOREAU

Robert Oakley Marshall: "Speed Demon on the Boulevard of Dreams"[1]

AFTER THE PROSECUTOR had summed up the case against their dad, and there could be no doubt in anyone's mind, not even their own, about the horrific fact that their father really had killed their mother, Roby and Chris, twenty and nineteen, were thinking the same thing. Their lives were a lie. They had always been envied, admired, privileged. They had had money and a perfect family. "How much in love with each other they'd all seemed. . . . The all-American family. The American Dream that came true."[2]

The sons now knew the truth: that their father, Rob, a spectacularly successful New Jersey life insurance salesman, had indeed arranged with professional assassins in Louisiana to come up on the night of September 7, 1984, to Atlantic City; that he had arranged the same night to drive his wife Maria to dinner at Harrah's in his Cadillac Eldorado. After dinner and wine and some late gambling in the casino, Rob had driven his sleepy wife back toward Toms River, had pulled off the parkway at the Oyster Creek picnic area to check out what he told Maria seemed to be a problem in the tire. Going out to check the tire, he had waited for the paid executioners to steal up to the car, assassinate Maria point blank in the back, swat Rob on the head to draw a little blood and make it look like a good robbery. (The Louisiana men had wanted to inflict a shooting wound but Rob had gone white and almost fainted — saying, "I'm not the one getting shot" — and insisted on getting only a flesh wound.) Rob had returned home looking strangely buoyant after his trauma, striking one detective as more like a man ready to go out sailing on his yacht than someone who had just lost his wife. He had reason to feel a large burden had been lifted from his shoulders; Rob Marshall now stood to recover approximately 1.5 million dollars of insurance money he had taken out on Maria, more than enough to clear $200,000 in gambling debts he owed in Atlantic City, and to set himself up handsomely for his next steps on the ladder of the American Dream. He could pay off the mortgage, buy a new car for himself and each of his three boys, and indulge in a whirlwind romance with his sexy mistress.

Rob Marshall had good cause to feel that the police would not come after him. Talking to Gene, his brother-in-law and a lawyer, who pointed out that it did not look especially good that Rob was deep in debt and stood to get such a huge insurance payment, Rob responded that the police could not possibly suspect him. "I'm much too high up the civic ladder. My reputation in the community, in fact, places me beyond reproach."[3]

He was right about one thing; the police themselves called Rob a "pillar" in the community. Back in the early seventies, Rob quickly proved himself a sensational salesman, selling over two million dollars in life insurance in his first year, and the next year he was again named among the top fifty Provident Mutual Life salesmen in the country. Rob and his family moved into a big house and Rob drove around town in a flashy red Cadillac. Rob had also scored big in his private life, capturing Maria, a Philadelphia Main Line doctor's wife who was exquisitely beautiful and who always kept herself and her sons impeccably groomed.[4] Maria was Rob's proudest possession. He loved her beauty. When he was arranging to have her killed, Rob told the executioners they must not mar Maria's looks; he could not stand that idea.

Rob and Maria, Joe McGinniss writes, were like royalty in Toms River. One neighbor said they "seemed to have the ideal family and lifestyle. You know, like you'd see on TV."[5] Everyone admired how they looked; they also admired Rob's business success and the fact that the Marshalls "were always buying something new." They moved to a bigger house, joined the country club. Maria was invited to join Laurel Twigs, a prestigious charitable organization, and Rob became a mover and shaker in the Rotary Club, the United Way, and the country club.[6]

There was not much doubt about how Rob had gotten so far so fast. The man was *driven*, the most aggressive salesman Toms River had ever seen. Kevin Kelly, the prosecutor who had once bought insurance from Rob, said Rob pushed through the deal while half his hamburger was still on his plate and the engine still hot in the parking lot. "The guy could fit in three or four lunches a day, the way he hustled." His drive — and his ego — seemed as big as Donald Trump's, who happened to own the Atlantic City casinos where Rob gambled and where he staged Maria's last supper.[7]

Over the course of his nationally publicized trial, later celebrated in the TV miniseries "Blind Faith," Rob's shameless behavior confirmed the nefarious picture of a sociopathic, greed-soaked personality painted by the prosecutor. In the first few weeks after the murder, Rob could barely conceal his excitement about his new freedom, not only making quick moves to get his hands on the money, but charming at least three different women into his wife's bed before he had figured out how to dispose of her remains. He staged a phony suicide attempt, giving himself the opportunity to leave "suicide tapes" by which he could publicly display his love of his kids and

Maria. The fact is, as prosecutor Kevin Kelly showed, nobody close to Rob ever heard him weep or saw him show any real grief or sense of loss over Maria. In fact, Rob had indifferently left her ashes in a brown cardboard box in a drawer in the funeral home, while at the same time he put back on and prominently wore at the trial the gold wedding ring Maria had given him. Rob would embarrass his sons by his public demonstrations of his love for them, wearing signs for the cameras saying "I love you," even as he was desperately urging them to perjure and risk jail to save his neck.

Prosecutor Kevin Kelly summed up Rob's personality: he's "self-centered, he's greedy, he's desperate, he's materialistic, and he's a liar. . . . he will use anybody, he will say anything, and he will do anything—including use his own family—to get out from under." Rob was single-mindedly out for number one; he "loves no one but himself."[8]

Kelly was not greatly exaggerating, but what he knew and did not say was that many of the same epithets could be written about many other Toms River residents. The fact is, as one native observed, Rob was in many ways not a whole lot different from his neighbors. Rob's case, one resident wrote, was compelling precisely because there was an intimate connection between "the town's collective values and the story of Rob and Maria Marshall." Indeed, the spotlight on Rob—and the community's obsession with it—stemmed from the fact that it helped to bring into sharp definition what the community was really about.[9]

Toms River in the 1970s was full of people in a hurry, many of them like the Marshalls, recent town immigrants scurrying to cash in on one of the biggest booms on the New Jersey shore. Ocean County was the second-fastest growing county in the country, causing real estate values to soar, and triggering spectacular business opportunities. The mostly blue collar and lower middle-class migrants that flocked to Toms River caught the fantastic entrepreneurial fever. Everyone in Toms River was suddenly making deals—and the limits on the money to be made evaporated. Since most people were new to the community, conspicuous consumption became the quickest way to get known and command respect. "I shop, therefore I am" became the Toms River credo long before it started showing up on bumper stickers around the country in the 1980s. Lots of other Toms River folks were joining the country club and driving their Cadillacs up to Atlantic City at night, joining Rob for the big bets at the high-priced blackjack tables.

Rob was a hustler, but hustling was the name of the game in Toms River—just as it was in Atlantic City and increasingly becoming in Ronald Reagan's Washington and on Wall Street. Rob, a number of commentators observed, was remarkably tuned in to the spirit of his times. The commercials about getting yours and getting it now kept ringing in his ears. And as the eighties progressed, Rob tuned in to bigger dreams than Toms River could offer. "See, all around Rob in the eighties," one old friend said, "everybody was scoring everything: sex, dope, big-money deals. At least, he thought so."[10] If those young kids out of business school could be making their first million on Wall Street before they were thirty, Rob was missing something he deserved. As his success grew, so did his aspirations, his sense of deprivation, and his gambling debts. Like the country as a whole, Rob was going to leverage himself into a real fortune.

Yet if the resonance between Rob and the collective values of his time was electric, most people in Toms River or Atlantic City were not murdering their wives to cover their debts and get one more step up the ladder. Rob *was* different, but mainly because he personified so purely and acted out so unrestrainedly the hungers driving his neighbors. Lots of others were dreaming the same big American Dream. But Rob was completely engulfed by it, his personality a machine perfectly dedicated to "making it." Rob was abnormal because the American Dream that was becoming the new standard had penetrated every fiber of his being, purging all traces of emotional or moral sensibilities that restrained his neighbors. Rob's aggressiveness was startling even in an age of hustlers, his narcissism was more extreme than most of his fellow travellers in the me generation, and in an age of moral decline, his conscience was exceptionally elastic.

Undoubtedly, Rob's "abnormality" had roots in his past; perhaps in the Depression, which ruined his family and turned his father into an alcoholic; perhaps in his chronic sense of being an outsider, having moved at least ten times before he was sixteen. But if Rob had not murdered his wife, he would never have come under the psychiatric microscope, because his extreme traits were exactly those that people on the way up were supposed to exhibit — and would propel them to the top. For fifteen years, Rob's "abnormality" had helped make him the biggest success in his community.

Rob got into trouble only because his dreams finally outstripped his own formidable capacities. He probably would not have killed Maria if he had not fallen so deeply into debt, and he might not have gotten into such debt if he had not been lured by the bigger dreams and looser moral sensibilities that his friends said had gotten under his skin and now possessed him. The reckless and grandiose entrepreneurial culture of Toms River that would later sweep across America released the extremes in Rob's personality, nurturing his sense of himself as a legend in his own time, free to make his own rules and look after number one first. When he got into deep financial trouble, the culture that might have restrained him was instead unleashing his deep-seated potential for wilding.

Them and Us

Public reaction to ultimate wilders like Rob Marshall has been schizophrenic. Utter shock that anyone could indifferently wipe out a wife, husband, mother or child "like an insect" for money is linked with a sliver of recognition that there is something familiar about these killers. "The first thing people want to know," Alison Bass wrote in the *Boston Globe*, is "how could anyone so carefully and coolly plan the murder of a wife, a child, anyone?"[11] But the second, usually subliminal, question is, "Could *my* husband do it?" or, even more subliminal, "Could I?"

Do ultimate wilders tell us something important about ourselves and our society—or are they bizarre sideshows? Reassuring responses come from the many commentators who observe, as does psychiatrist Dr. Charles Ford, that while people like Rob Marshall "on the surface look very normal," they are suffering from mental illness or deep-seated "character disorders," such as narcissism or sociopathy, that radically differentiate "them" from "us."[12] Criminologists Jack Levin and James Fox describe sociopaths like Marshall and his remarkably similar fellow wilder, Charles Stuart, as people who "blend in well and function appropriately" but are "far from normal." The criminologists explain that sociopaths "know the right thing to do" to emulate the rest of us; they are consummate actors: "Sociopaths lie, manipulate, and deceive. They are *good* at it. Like actors they play a role on the stage of life. . . . "[13]

When they murder, ultimate wilders clearly *act* differently, but the clinical accounts of their "character disorders" do not provide a persuasive argument for the difference between "them" and "us." The bible of psychiatry, the *Diagnostic Standard Manual* defines narcissistic personality disorder as "The tendency to exploit others to achieve one's own ends, to exaggerate achievements and talents, to feel entitled to and to crave constant attention and adulation."[14] Criminologists Fox and Levin define sociopaths as "self-centered, manipulative, possessive, envious, reckless, and unreliable. They demand special treatment and inordinate attention, often exaggerating their own importance. . . . On their way to the top, sociopaths ruthlessly step over their competitors without shame or guilt." These seem among the most common of human frailties, and Fox and Levin acknowledge that they are widespread among Americans, who live in a culture that often idolizes characters such as J. R. Ewing of "Dallas," the personification of virtually all the sociopathic traits. In trying to predict when sociopaths will actually turn to murder—the one tangible difference between "them" and "us"—Fox and Levin end up in another conundrum, for they acknowledge that most sociopaths rarely reach the point "at which they feel it necessary to kill. Most of them live ordinary lives." Distinguishing "them" from "us" then seems a bit like the dilemma American soldiers faced in Vietnam, trying to distinguish the guerillas from the rest of the population.

It is time for sociologists to reclaim the idea of sociopathy, a concept as useful for understanding a diseased society as the sick psyche. A sociopathic society is one, like the Ik, marked by a collapse of moral order, reflecting the breakdown of community and the failure of institutions responsible for inspiring moral vision and creating and enforcing robust moral codes. In such a society, the national character type tends toward sociopathy, and idealized behavior, while veiled in a rhetoric of morality, becomes blurred with antisocial egoism. The founders of modern sociology, especially Émile Durkheim, worried that modernity threatened to turn the most developed industrial cultures into sociopathic caldrons, conceiving the sociological enterprise as an effort to understand how societies could find their moral compass and preserve themselves in the face of the sociopathic threat.

In sociopathic societies, the clinical effort to dissect the sociopathic personality cannot be separated from an analysis of national character and ideology. Rob Marshall may be deranged, but his derangement mirrors a national disorder. In the United States, as it approaches the twenty-first century, the official religion of the "free market" increasingly sanctifies sociopathy under the guise of individual initiative, entrepreneurship, and "making it." As the American Dream becomes a recipe for wilding, clinicians and criminologists need to deepen their sociological understanding, or they will continue to misread Rob Marshall as a failure of socialization rather than a pathology of "oversocialization." Rob had internalized *too* deeply the central American values of competitiveness and material success, discarding any other values that might interfere. Rob is most interesting as a prisoner of the same American Dream that compels the rest of us but does not consume us with quite the same intensity.

Lyle and Erik Menendez: A Family of Competitors

At the time of this writing, Lyle and Erik Menendez have been charged with murder, but have yet to stand trial. I reconstruct the case below from public accounts.

On the evening of August 20, 1989, as José Menendez was watching television in the spacious den of his $4 million Beverly Hills estate, he had reason to feel pretty good about his life. José was a perfectionist who, according to his older son, Lyle, felt he could never "do something well enough." But even José, with his high standards and his consuming ambition, might admit that an impoverished immigrant who by age forty-five had risen to become a millionaire in Hollywood's inner sanctum had not done too badly. He could count Hollywood celebrities Rick Springfield, Barry Manilow, Kenny Rogers, and Sylvester Stallone as his friends. Founder and president of Live Entertainment, Inc., a successful national video-cassette distributor, his was a Horatio Alger story come true. Journalist Pete Hammill wrote in *Esquire* magazine that José was a "glittering" testimony to the American Dream of the Reagan years.[15]

As he sat with his wife Kitty that evening eating fresh berries and cream, José would certainly have gotten deep satisfaction from the comments of his fellow executive Ralph King, who eulogized José in the *Wall Street Journal* after his death as "by far the brightest, toughest businessman I have ever worked with," or of former Hertz chairman Robert Stone, who said he "had never known anyone who worked harder, worked to-ward more goals." José, according to Stone, probably "would have become president of the company" had he stayed at Hertz. Coming to the United States from Cuba at age fifteen, José had dedicated every ounce of his being to getting ahead, vowing to "develop strip malls," if that was what it took to "succeed by age thirty." He could not have been better psychologically equipped. He was an intensely aggressive and competitive man brimming with entrepreneurial energy. Out of accounting school, he had hustled from Coopers and Lybrand to a Chicago shipping firm to Hertz, and then to RCA, successfully signing on performer José Feliciano. After being passed over for executive vice-president at RCA, José achieved a brilliant coup by creating Live Entertainment, Inc. as the video arm of Carolco Pictures, on whose board he sat and which had gone big-time with its smash hit, *Rambo II*.[16]

Turning to his two handsome sons as they burst into the room, José could savor a different kind of pride. José had a burning desire to see his sons succeed as he had, and he had dedicated himself to that end with the same relentless passion with which he had pursued his business goals, drilling Lyle and Erik for hours on the tennis courts and constantly exhorting them to outcompete their peers on and off the court. "There is a lot of pressure," Erik said, "to be great." Now, Lyle, aged twenty-two, was to graduate soon from Princeton, and José's younger son, Erik, aged nineteen, who had gotten into UCLA, was talking about wanting to realize his father's own ambition of becoming the first Cuban-American U.S. senator.

José was probably more puzzled than frightened when he saw that Lyle and Erik were both carrying shotguns. But he had no time to ask questions. Within seconds of barging into the den, as police reconstruct the scene, the two sons had fired eight shots point blank at their father, and five at their mother. Just to make sure, they thrust the barrel of one gun into their father's mouth and blew off the back of his head. Police would later say that the murder scene was so gruesome that it could

not possibly have been a Mafia hit, as some had first speculated, for the Mob kills "clean." As Erik told reporters after the
crime, his parents' ravaged, bloodspattered, lifeless bodies
"looked like wax."[17]

Lyle and Erik claimed that they had gone out that evening
to see the James Bond film *License to Kill*, but ended up seeing
Batman. They came back late at night, they said, horrified to
find the carnage at home. Neighbors reported that they heard
the sons screaming and sobbing, presumably after discovering
the bodies. But police suspected Lyle and Erik from the very
beginning, and not only because, as District Attorney Ira
Reiner put it, a $14 million estate provided "an ample motive."
The boys were not able to produce ticket stubs for *Batman*, and
police had found a shotgun shell casing in one of Lyle's jackets.
Then investigators discovered that two years earlier in high
school Erik had cowritten a play about a wealthy teenager who
murders his parents for money, a creation that made his mother, who helped type the manuscript, feel proud of her son's
gifts. But it was about six months later, in early March 1990,
that police found the smoking pistol they were seeking, when
they confiscated tapes of psychotherapy sessions with both boys
which apparently offered direct evidence of their involvement
in the crime.

"Why Would Brothers Who Had Everything Murder Their
Parents?" ran the *Wall Street Journal* headline, posing the question that journalists all over the country began to probe. A
carefully calculated double parricide seems almost unfathoma-
ble even in the most brutal of families, and the Menendez family was believed by friends and relatives to be "close and
loving." Friends reported Kitty to be a "supportive mother"
who attended virtually all of her sons' many tennis and other
athletic competitions. José had driven them hard, but he was
a deeply devoted father, spending hours with his sons and indulging them with extravagances, such as Lyle's red Alfa
Romeo and expensive Italian clothing. When Lyle was disciplined at Princeton for plagiarism, his father came across

country to defend him, "more upset at the school than at Lyle." There were family squabbles, friends said, like José's and Kitty's unhappiness about a girl Lyle was seeing, but nothing out of the ordinary.[18]

Neither son showed evidence of a serious clinical pathology that could explain a tendency to murder. Friends and relatives described the brothers as outgoing and "extremely self-assured." Their assertiveness and confidence, to some, bordered on arrogance. One friend said he was attracted to Erik by a "shared sense that we were special. . . . People looked up to us," Craig Cignarelli, a coauthor of the murder play, said, "We have an aura of superiority." Their parents' wealth and indulgence had turned the boys into "brats," according to some friends of the family, but nobody saw them as psychotic or deeply neurotic. It is implausible that *both* boys could have been psychotic without anyone noticing. Media reports suggest a picture of very intense and ambitious young men with a zest for life and a rebellious spirit.[19]

The remarkable behavior of Lyle and Erik after the murders offers the most revealing clues to why they committed them. Neither boy wasted any time. Lyle dropped out of Princeton and, after flirting with the idea of a professional tennis career (he had once ranked thirty-sixth in the U.S. juniors), decided "to build a business empire from the ground up." Taking his share of an initial $400,000 insurance payment, he bought Chuck's Spring Street Cafe, a popular student hangout around the Princeton campus specializing in fried chicken. Lyle immediately began drafting plans to open franchises in other states as part of a nationwide chain. His entrepreneurial ambitions extended far beyond restaurants. Lyle began traveling widely to help realize his dream of making "a fortune in, among other things, show business and real estate." He founded Investment Enterprises, a financing shell for channeling the millions of dollars he would inherit into quick high-yield returns.[20]

As for Erik, he was serious about pro tennis, immediately dropping out of UCLA and hiring a professional tennis coach for $50,000 a year. He moved into the exclusive Marina City Club Towers, a glamorous ocean-side setting south of Los Angeles. Erik worked as hard at his tennis career as Lyle did in his restaurant and real estate ventures, practicing for hours on the court and taking his coach along to boost his performance in tournaments. Erik, however, did not limit himself to a future in tennis. Still proud of his earlier murder script, Erik believed he had a spectacular future as a screenwriter. In his spare time, he worked on his plays and poetry. He told his roommate at Marina that he was confident he would "produce an unbelievable script."[21]

It took little imagination to view the murders, as the police did, as a grand entrepreneurial scheme, ironically a testimony to the grip of their father's own deepest values on the minds of his sons. José had wanted, more than anything else, Erik and Lyle to follow in his footsteps and live out the American Dream that had guided his own life. He had raised them to be aggressive competitors like himself who would seize every opportunity to get ahead and make something of themselves. "He wanted us," Erik said, "to be exactly like him." Lyle and Erik converted parricide into a carefully planned strategy for catapulting their careers into fast forward. In a bizarre twist they proved how fully they had imbibed their father's values and opened themselves to the entrepreneurial spirit of the decade that shaped them.[22]

Lyle and Erik were themselves fully aware of the power of the ties to the father they killed. "We are prototypes of my father," Erik pronounced after the murder. He added, "I'm not going to live my life for my father, but I think his dreams are what I want to achieve. I feel he's in me, pushing me." As for Lyle, he all but admitted that his whole life had been a preparation for the day when he could jump into his father's shoes. Two days after the murder, Lyle told his friend, Glen Stevens, who commented on how well he seemed to be holding up, "I've been waiting so long to be in this position." Later, commenting on his ambitious business plans Lyle said, "I just entered into my father's mode."[23]

The Menendez brothers had become prisoners of the American Dream, captives of their father's extravagant ambitions. Theirs may have been "ambition gone berserk," as a *Wall Street Journal* reporter put it, but it represented less a crazy break from reality than an excessive vulnerability to the culture around them. The messages coming from their father, from Beverly Hills, from Princeton, from Wall Street, and, as we shall see, from both the Reagan and Bush White House were telling them the same thing: Money is good, more money is better, and they had only themselves to blame if they did not seize every opportunity to strike it rich. The seductive power of these messages on the boys is apparent in their uncontrollable orgasm of spending after getting the first cut of their inheritance. Lyle bought a new Porsche, not especially unusual, but his spending on clothes was extravagant, even for Princeton. Upscale clothier Stuart Lindner remembers Lyle coming into his store "dressed in an expensive black cashmere jacket and wearing a Rolex watch," which Lindner priced at about $15,000. On that occasion, Lyle bought about $600 worth of clothes, including five ninety-dollar silk shirts. "We've had bigger sales," Lindner said, "but not in four minutes."[24]

The sons worshipped the same God as their father, but they gave the family religion a 1980s spin. They had grown up in the era of Donald Trump and Ivan Boesky, who made their father's career seem slow and his fortune paltry. Lyle told Venanzia Momo, owner of a Princeton pizza parlor Lyle tried to buy, that he did not want to have to struggle like his father did to succeed. "He said he wanted to do it faster and quicker," Momo said. "He said he had a better way."[25]

Seeds of Lyle's and Erik's ultimate wilding could be seen in a trail of small wildings, reflecting the casual morality of the quick money culture that engulfed them. Even as an adolescent, Lyle frequently went on spending binges, once running up a huge hotel bill in Tucson that his father had to cover. He racked up so many traffic violations that his license was suspended twice, and several times he got into trouble with the police during his travels in Italy. At Princeton, he copied a lab report of a fellow psychology student and was told he could leave voluntarily or be expelled. Meanwhile, Erik also brushed with the law, ending up in juvenile court on a number of occasions. José, however, was always there to bail the boys out, a perhaps fatal source of support, for it may well have been that their success in getting out of small jams helped persuade them that they could also get away with murder.

The Menendez murder "speaks to every parent," says television producer Steven White. "Matricide and patricide go back to Greek drama." But Lyle and Erik are poignant products of America in 1990. Their abnormality lies most of all in their uncritical receptivity to the "look after number one" message at the heart of American life. Lyle's and Erik's pathology was that they allowed themselves to be socialized so completely. They lacked the capacity to resist their father's dreams and the mesmerizing money obsession of the Reagan-Bush era. What José had not realized was that it was not his children's ambition he had to cultivate — the larger culture would see to that — but the tender sentiments and moral sensibilities that might have prevented their ambition from metastasizing into a cancer of wilding.

Then and Now

In 1925, *An American Tragedy* by Theodore Dreiser was published. One of the country's great works of literature, it is about a young man, Clyde Griffiths, who plots to kill his pregnant girlfriend, Roberta, so that he can take up with a woman who is rich and well connected. The story is based on a real murder committed in 1906 by Chester Gillette, a New Yorker who drowned his pregnant girlfriend to be free to pursue a woman in high society. The striking resemblance of Dreiser's hero to

Lyle and Erik Menendez, and to other contemporary men in a hurry like Rob Marshall and Charles Stuart, suggests that wilding, even ultimate wilding, is not new. But if the parallels tell us something important about the deep historical roots of American wilding, there are also noteworthy contrasts that hint at how the virus has mutated for the worse.

Like Erik and Lyle, Clyde was an authentic prisoner of the American Dream (as was presumably the real Chester Gillette, for as H. L. Mencken notes, Dreiser stayed "close to the facts" and came close to "literal reporting"). When Dreiser describes Clyde as "bewitched" by wealth, a "personification of desire" for all the glitter and beauty that money can buy, he could not have better described Erik and Lyle. Indeed, Dreiser sees young Clyde as so vulnerable to the seductive temptations that surrounded him, so "helpless" in the face of the material pleasures just beyond his reach, that he asks whether the real guilt for the crime lay not with Clyde but with the culture that has debased him. No doubt future novelists or historians could instructively engage the same questions about the Menendez brothers, whose vulnerability to modern capitalist seductions is one of the most poignant aspects of their identity.

Dreiser selected the Gillette case, as critic Lawrence Hussman informs us, because he saw it as "typical enough to warrant treatment as particularly American." Dreiser recognized that whatever psychological pathology was involved could only be understood in the context of a diagnosis of the health of American society and an inquiry into the moral ambiguity of the American Dream. *An American Tragedy* was compelling to millions of Americans in the 1920s because it held up a mirror in which they could see their collective reflection. The novel's success suggests that there was something of Clyde in many Americans of his era, which tells us how deeply the wilding virus had already insinuated itself into American life. Indeed, as early as the Robber Baron era of the late 1800s, the wilding streak in American culture had become too obvious to ignore,

a matter of preoccupation for satirist Mark Twain, philosopher
Henry David Thoreau, and the critic Lincoln Steffens.[26]

Yet if Dreiser's work suggests that wilding defines a con-
tinuity, not a break, in American life, it also hints at how things
have changed. Unlike Rob Marshall or Erik and Lyle, Clyde
could not actually go through with his diabolical scheme. After
becoming obsessed with plans to kill his girlfriend, he lures her
into a canoe with the intent of drowning her, but, whether out
of weakness or moral compunction, he cannot do it. His problem is solved only because she accidentally falls into the water,
along with Clyde himself. Clyde does not try to save her, partly
out of fear that her thrashing about will drown him too, but
that is quite different from deliberate murder. Perhaps in the
America of 1925, it was still not credible to Dreiser or his audience that anyone could actually carry out such a crime, although the real Chester Gillette was only one of a number of
such accused killers in the first quarter of the twentieth century.
While such murders still shock the public, Americans today,
according to pollsters, not only believe that such crimes can be
committed but, as noted earlier, worry whether their spouses,
or they themselves, could succumb to the impulse. It is also
noteworthy that Woody Allen has his modern-day fictional
Clyde, Dr. Judah, follow through on his murderous plot at the
point that Clyde pulled back.

That the constraints on wilding may have weakened over
the last seventy-five years is suggested further by the centrality
of the theme of guilt and moral responsibility in Dreiser's work.
Clyde is a morally weak character, but he is not entirely devoid
of conscience. After Roberta's death, Clyde is not able to ab-
solve himself of responsibility, plagued by the question of
whether he was guilty of not trying to save her. In contrast,
Woody Allen's Dr. Judah rationalizes his mistress's murder as
one of life's necessary moral compromises and soon returns to
his normal life perfectly free of guilt. Perhaps the most extraordinary aspect of Rob Marshall and the Menendez brothers is
their apparent lack of remorse. Friends of Rob, Erik and Lyle,

and Charles Stuart, too, commented on how well they looked after the murders; indeed, they all seemed happier and better adjusted after their crimes and never appeared to suffer even twinges of conscience.

Dreiser's *An American Tragedy* is ultimately an indictment of the American Dream. The "primary message of the book," Lawrence Hussman reminds us, concerns the "destructive materialistic goals" that obsess Clyde and drive him to his murderous plot. Dreiser refused to accept that the evil could be explained simply by Clyde's moral weakness or some presumed individual psychopathology; it was only the inability to question "some of the basic assumptions on which American society is based" that could lead anyone to that line of thinking. Dreiser himself concluded that Clyde had to be held morally accountable, but that society was the ultimate perpetrator of the crime. He implicitly instructs his readers that such American tragedies would recur until the country finally triumphed over its obsessions with materialism and ego and rediscovered its moral compass.

Dreiser's musings on the American Dream remain stunningly relevant today, and the book is an eerie prophecy of current cases of wilding. But if Dreiser saw how the American Dream of his era could beget extreme individual wilding, he could not have foreseen the historical developments that have made the dream a recipe for a wilding epidemic. In his day, the "American Century" was dawning on a glorious future; the prosperity of the twenties was just a harbinger of a new era of plenty, in which all Americans could reasonably look forward to their share of an apparently endlessly expanding American pie. Despite the dark side of the materialistic preoccupation, which divided people as they competed for the biggest slices, the dream also brought Americans together, for as long as the pie was growing, everybody could win.

It took a new age of limits and decline, when growing numbers of Americans would see their share of the pie shrinking and others were permanently removed from the table, to set the stage for a full-blown wilding epidemic. Dreiser saw a fore-shadowing of this in the Great Depression, which turned him toward socialism. But America pulled together in the thirties and the wilding virus was kept largely in check, as I discuss in Chapter 7. It would take a very different set of economic and political reversals, half a century later, to fuel the kind of wilding epidemic that Dreiser vaguely anticipated but never experienced.

It is apt testimony to Dreiser, as well as to the ferocious spread of the epidemic he could only dimly envisage, to mention in conclusion the rapidly growing crowd of modern-day Chester Gillettes. In addition to Rob Marshall and the Menendez brothers, Charles Stuart is, perhaps, the most remarkable Gillette "look-alike," not only because he killed his pregnant wife, but because, like Chester, he was from a working-class background and disposed of his wife because she had become an impediment to his moving up. Stuart, of course, trumped Gillette's achievement by collecting several hundred thousand dollars in insurance money. As did Kenneth Johnson, a New Hampshire carpenter with a taste for the high life, who paid two teenagers $5,000 each to kill *his* pregnant wife just a few months before the Stuart murder, and collected thousands of dollars in pension and insurance money.

Getting much more publicity than Johnson was his fellow New Hampshire resident Pamela Smart, a young, ambitious media services director in the public school system who said she dreamed of becoming the next Barbara Walters. Dubbed the "ice princess" because of her public demeanor, Smart had the same drive as Rob Marshall. She was an honors student in high school and college and a cheerleader. In 1991, Smart was convicted of seducing a teenager to help kill her husband; her motives included the desire to pocket $140,000 in insurance money. It is unclear whether there were any female Chester Gillettes in Dreiser's day, but that women no longer have any immunity is proved by such convicted killers as Marie Hilary, whose successful poisoning of her husband and attempted poisoning of her daughter for insurance money, earned her national publicity and the title of the "black widow" from the prosecuting attorney. At the time of Smart's conviction, another young woman in Detroit, Toni Cato Riggs, was charged with masterminding the murder of *her* husband for insurance money. Riggs' soldier husband had just returned from service in the Gulf war.[27]

This rogues' list is just the tip of the iceberg, not only of the larger wilding epidemic but of the roster of ultimate wilders, male and female, rich and poor, who are now grabbing headlines. Experts conservatively estimate that hundreds of such calculated, cold-blooded family murders for money have taken place in the past decade. What is striking is not just the numbers, but the percentage of those who were described by friends, associates, and the police as all-American types, defying all suspicion because they so purely embodied the qualities and the success that Americans idealize. This leads us from the ultimate wilders themselves to the figures and forces in society that give rise to the wilding epidemic. These include, as we see in the next two chapters, some of the most prominent politicians and business leaders in America, as well as some of America's most cherished institutions.

3

A Fish Rots from
the Head First
Washington and Wall Street
Go Wild: I

Bad money drives out good.
HENRY DUNNING MACLEOD

PRESIDENT REAGAN singled out one book that he said helped inspire his vision for America. The book was *Wealth and Poverty* by neoconservative writer George Gilder. Speaking on television, Reagan held up Gilder's book and hailed its vision of a new American hero, the *entrepreneur*. Gilder had a bold and romantic script for helping America stand tall again, but it also proved to be a recipe for wilding. Born in the magical womb of Reaganomics, the new entrepreneur turned out to be an economic wilder, a deregulated personality in hot pursuit of fast fortune, who would help rewrite the American Dream.

Gilder celebrated men like Nick Kelley in Lee, Massachusetts, whose entrepreneurial juices began to stir as a sophomore in college when he got upset by the reams of wasted paper he saw on the floor of his stepfather's papermaking-machine factory. Kelley figured out a new way to manufacture scratch pads from the paper his stepfather would normally throw in the Lee dump. He overcame serious technical and financial problems to create a thriving scratch pad business. But when he realized he could not compete with an ingenious Italian family of scratch pad producers in Somerville, Massachussetts, Nick adapted. He bought scratch pads from his competitors and began decorating them with emblems, turning some into

43

legal pads. Then he found he could process tea bags from the paper, a creative breakthrough that led other papermaking companies to channel difficult projects to him. Eventually, he started three successful new businesses: one making women's fingernail mending tissue for firms like Avon and Revlon; another manufacturing facial blotting tissue for companies like Mary Kaye and Bonne Belle; and the most successful, creating extremely thin, lint-free papers for wrapping silicon wafers utilized by the computer industry.[1]

Nick Kelley, like other successful entrepreneurs, had a passion for money — and made a lot of it. Gilder describes Kelley's drive to make money as a "gift" to society. Making money, according to Gilder, is the most important gift anyone can give in a market economy. Capitalism, Gilder writes, "begins with giving." Entrepreneurs like Kelley, by investing their time, creativity, and money in projects without any sure return, are running risks for the well-being of others. Without their initiative and willingness to run such risks, capitalist economies would go belly-up.

The entrepreneur's contribution is as much spiritual as economic. Gilder sees the self-interest of the entrepreneur as holy, endowing it with a deep moral and religious significance. The entrepreneur's gift of investment in an uncertain market affirms the most important faith a society can have — "Faith in one's neighbors, in one's society, and in the compensatory logic of the cosmos." The entrepreneur "does not make gifts [that is, invest]," Gilder tells us, "without some sense, possibly unconscious, that one will be rewarded, whether in this world or the next. Even the biblical injunction affirms that the giver will be given unto."[2]

The entrepreneur, Gilder writes, is a great figure. Life is an "adventure" in which the entrepreneur "participates with a heightened consciousness and passion and an alertness and diligence that greatly enhance his experience of learning." Even the entrepreneur's failures are societal successes because they generate "knowledge of a deeper kind than is taught in schools or acquired in the controlled experiments of social or physical science"—knowledge that "is the crucial source of creativity and initiative in any economic system."[3]

George Gilder's hero was also Ronald Reagan's. Reagan proclaimed:

> Those who say that we're living in a time when there are no heroes—they just don't where to look . . . There are entrepreneurs with faith in themselves and faith in an idea, who create new jobs, new wealth, and new opportunities. It is time to realize that we are too great a nation to limit ourselves to small dreams."[4]

It was America's genius, Reagan said, to produce thousands of entrepreneurs who had big lusty dreams for themselves and their country. "Their spirit is as big as the universe," Reagan proclaimed in his inaugural address, and "their hearts are bigger than their spirit." They were tough, ambitious, generous individuals whose restless dynamism was the high octane gasoline in America's economic engine. Their dream—synonymous with Ronald Reagan's American Dream—was to make themselves rich and the country rich.

Yes, the entrepreneur may be driven by a large appetite for money and power. But Reagan, with his perennial optimism and his own reading of American history, assured the public that only good could come from unleashing the primal urge for self-aggrandizement. The magic of the market was that it directed the selfish energies of the entrepreneur into socially productive channels, yielding the bonanza of modern American capitalism. It was thus that Reagan could proclaim without any hesitation, "What I want to see above all else is that this remains a country where someone can always get rich."[5]

Reagan proceeded to engineer his own perestroika on the American economy, designed to liberate the entrepreneur and ensure that he or she "can always get rich." Over a compliant Congress that too readily acquiesced to his radical program (reflecting the new power of big business over Democratic Party financing), Reagan waved his magic wand in two decisive strokes, one deregulating almost the entire economy and thus freeing the entrepreneur from unwelcome government controls, another cutting taxes on the wealthy to ensure entrepreneurs their pots of gold would not be taken away from them. Just as important, Reagan lost no time demonstrating through example his high regard for the rich. He surrounded himself with a kitchen cabinet of wealthy entrepreneurs, like beer magnate Alfred Coors. And at the outset of his administration, he threw the most opulent inauguration party in history: a four day $11 million celebration involving nine formal balls, a fireworks display of 10,000 rockets, and a parade of white ties, limousines, and minks that prompted even Arizona's conservative Senator Barry Goldwater to complain about such an "ostentatious" display "at a time when most people can't hack it." At one of the inaugural balls, Frank Sinatra, accurately sniffing the winds of the new administration, crooned to Nancy Reagan: "I'm so proud that you're First Lady Nancy/ And so pleased that I'm sort of a chum/ The next eight years will be fancy/ As fancy as they come."[6]

The myth of entrepreneurship and the celebration of the rich is, again, nothing new in American history. Reaganism is only the latest stage in the long saga of America's economic individualism that mythologizes self-made heroes and celebrates entrepreneurial initiative as the national religion. America's "rags to riches" legend, popularized by nineteenth-century novelist Horatio Alger, goes back to colonial days, surfacing in Ben Franklin's homespun *Poor Richard's Almanac*. Reagan's rhetoric clicked with the American people partly because it *was* so established in American tradition. The wilding forces that Reagan fired up have been germinating for decades in America's market economy and fiercely individualistic culture. Economic wilding, it should be clear, did not begin with Reaganism, nor will it end with Bushism or a new Democratic regime, for the problem lies deeper than any government can, by itself, create or cure.

But if Reaganism is only part of a longer story, it merits attention as an innovative chapter, because it decisively blurred the often tenuous line between American individualism and wilding. After the excesses of the Robber Barons and the Gilded Age, and the agonies of the depression, America recognized the shadowy side of the market and the moral ambiguities of the unregulated market. What made Ronald Reagan revolutionary was his capacity to see the world with the eyes of a mid-nineteenth-century cowboy or an eighteenth-century economist. Capitalism looked much to him as it had to Adam Smith when he described the famous "invisible hand" that ensured profit-seekers in the market would do good for society as well as themselves. Rhetorically championing the entrepreneur's high morality, Reagan resurrected a doctrine created for the world in 1776 as the manifesto for America going into the twenty-first century.

History would, however, play a cruel trick on America. First, Reagan's policies did not exactly square with his rhetoric, for it was not the struggling entrepreneur but the entrenched wealthy elite who reaped the bonanzas of the Reagan years; as conservative columnist Scott Burns wrote, "The facts suggest that the eighties will be known as the decade of the fat cats, a time when entrepreneurial pieties were used to beat the average worker into cowed submission while America's corporate elite moved yet higher on the hog." Kevin Phillips, perhaps the country's leading conservative analyst, agrees: "The 1980s saw upper-bracket America pull farther ahead of the rest of the nation . . . No parallel upsurge of riches has been seen since the late nineteenth century." The country's 400 wealthiest families tripled their net worth, Phillips shows, and the "trickle-down" effect predicted by conservative economists never seemed to occur: income in the hands of the country's richest 1 percent increased almost 50 percent while the poorest 20 percent of the population lost ground, claiming only 1 percent of the country's pretax national income.[7]

The rich prospered under Reagan because the Great Communicator never permitted his rhetorical devotion to the "free market" to inhibit his underwriting of government welfare for the wealthy. Reagan's "market revolution" was always a selective affair, exposing most of the working population to greater market insecurities, while extending corporate elites massive government protection. Welfare statism for the rich took the forms, among others, of increasing federal loan guarantees for banks (thus taking away the risks of speculation legalized by deregulation) and subsidizing industries through unprecedented tax breaks and risk-free government contracts, including billions of dollars of Pentagon contracts in the state planning system that Noam Chomsky and others aptly dub "military Keynesianism." Indeed, Chomsky argues that the administration "had only contempt for the 'invisible hand' and free market doctrine, and had no faith in entrepreneurs. They wanted the state to act to eliminate risk, transfer wealth to the rich, subsidize the functional parts of industry and agriculture and protect them from imports." Chomsky concludes that the Reaganites were actually "radical statists," who masked blatant use of government to support the rich with the ideology of market conservatism.[8]

The Reagnite religion of self-interest and "free market" — one of the most powerful ideological forces feeding the culture of wilding — was thus accompanied by a cynical pragmatism in policy, with the president and his men quite prepared to rely on either government or the market as necessary to advance their own interests. Reagan did, however, sponsor his own entrepreneurial revolution, liberating the "paper entrepreneur," a new species born in the wild and woolly womb of a radically deregulated money economy. In previous generations, American entrepreneurs had to produce or trade in goods that people actually could use. Reagan made it possible to make a fortune without producing anything of value. Paper entrepreneurs are lawyers, financiers, real estate speculators, investment bankers, and others who make money through financial transactions that do not increase the economic pie (although they sometimes contribute to rational restructuring of corporations) but, in Robert Reich's words, only "rearrange its slices." They are takeover artists (who buy and sell companies), "white knights" (who save companies from hostile takeovers), junk bond salesmen (peddling risky high-yield corporate bonds), "greenmailers" (who make money by threatening to buy companies), and others knowledgeable in the arcane arts of modern high finance. Because they can make millions overnight for themselves and their clients through skillful "rearranging" on the commodities exchanges or the merger and acquisition markets, paper entrepreneurs rapidly became dominant figures. Reich proclaimed unequivocally in 1988 that "the paper entrepreneurs are winning out over the product entrepreneurs."[9]

Paper Entrepreneurs are the ultimate economic wilders. Their enterprises proved inherently corrupt, not simply because they are dedicated to the dubious art of making quick windfalls, but because they are founded on the effort to make money without necessarily creating anything useful. President Reagan fervently believed that the unfettered market and his new entrepreneurs would simultaneously solve the nation's economic and moral crises. Instead, Reagan and his paper entrepreneurs made both problems worse. The paper entrepreneurs helped to rewrite the American Dream as the art of economic wilding, teaching thousands of admiring and envious young Americans that it was still possible to get rich if one did not permit moral sensibilities to interfere. As a case in point, consider the career of the country's leading paper entrepreneur.

Michael Milken: Billionaire King of Junk

Members of the group were talking about Michael Milken. One said, "We owe it all to one man and we are extraneous." Another joined in, more grandly, "Michael is the most important individual who has lived in this century." A third added,

"Someone like Michael comes along once every five hundred years."[10]

They sounded like the members of a 1960s cult, but these were savvy millionaire participants in one of the most high-powered investment groups in America, the "junk bond" department of Drexel Burnham Lambert Group, Inc. And they were talking about someone who, if not the most important figure of the last five hundred years, was indeed one of the giants of the 1980s. Richer and much more important than Donald Trump, he was Michael Milken, the founder and head of Drexel's awesome "junk bond" empire, who started a revolution in Wall Street — and ultimately the whole American economy — by virtually inventing the junk bond market. Junk bonds were discounted high-risk, high-yield bonds that had been around for years, but in Milken's hands they became the ultimate instrument of the takeover artist, the greenmailer and the arbitrager, making possible the brand new world of 1980s finance. Milken, who by age forty was said to personally control a junk bond market worth one hundred billion dollars, can be called the ultimate paper entrepreneur, the entrepreneur whose creation was paper entrepreneurship itself.

Milken drew on the theory of an unknown researcher, W. Braddock Hickman, who had studied the performance of low-grade bonds from 1900 to 1943 and discovered that they outperformed more traditional high-grade bonds. In other words, junk bonds were anything but junk (Milken would regret calling "the stuff junk," a friend later saying, "Mike would kill to have everybody know it as a high-yield bond"). Milken became an evangelist for junk. One buyer remembered that when Michael was selling junk, he was not like a trader selling bonds, he was "a messiah, preaching the gospel." Milken spent the first part of his career figuring out which down-and-out companies, like Penn Central, had low-grade bonds worth snapping up. But his inspiration came later, in marrying junk bonds to leveraged buyouts and other forms of "creative debt." Milken saw that if you wanted to buy a company and did not have the money, junk bonds were the way to go. Or if you were a low-grade company (one assigned a poor credit rating by Standard and Poors or other certifying agencies) and needed to raise money, junk was the way to go. Junk, Milken figured out, was the paper entrepreneur's perfect plastic card, the way to buy yourself out of any predicament or into any fast deal. All the paper entrepreneur needed was the will; Milken would arrange the rest.[11]

The "high-grade bond guys considered him a leper," but by the late 1970s Milken was making millions and so were his clients. A brilliant and obsessive student of companies, nobody knew the junk market like Milken did. Pretty soon, it became impossible to deal in junk bonds without dealing with him. By the mid-1980s, when junk had become the grease for virtually every acquisition deal on Wall Street, Mike was the man who had to cut your deal. He had 70 percent of the entire junk market. One client said, "Where was Morgan? Nowhere. Who's the only one who can tell you what's going on? Mike. So you go crawling on your knees." Another described Milken as like "a god in that end of the business and a god can do anything it wants." There were the new movers and shakers, like Carl Icahn and Henry Kravis and Rupert Murdoch, but the man creating these new "empire-builders," as Milken's business biographer, Connie Bruck, writes, "choosing them, molding them, sitting on their boards, owning pieces of their growing companies," was Michael Milken. At Drexel, when people asked for Michael, the secretary would indicate in hushed tones the whereabouts of the King.[12]

Milken became a legend in the business community. One of his business associates said, "I'm not much given to hero worship, but I have to tell you I never thought there would be a Michael Milken." Milken did for business what Donald Trump did for the general public: inspire faith in a new expansive and romantic American Dream tailored for the Reagan era and beyond. One Milken colleague, who originally planned to get a doctorate in history, proclaimed he was now not studying history but *making* it:

> When I read Alvin Toffler's *Future Shock*, and he described this vortex of change that whirls around us, and it happens very fast in New York City, and slower in Des Moines, and even slower in the outback of Australia, the thing that was amazing to me was, when I looked at the funnel of that maelstrom, the vortex of that sits right in the middle of my desk. I am the fella who determines what the changes will be. If I don't finance it, it ain't gonna happen. I get to decide who's going to get capital, to make the future. Now, I ask you — what's more romantic than that?[13]

While Milken initially terrorized "the older stuffier world of Ivily-degreed bankers and terminally tweeded fund managers," by the mid-1980s, he had given businesses a new entrepreneurial identity to hang their hats on — one, however, that put wilding at the heart of American enterprise.[14]

On April 25, 1990, the King appeared in a New York City courtroom and tearfully confessed that he had committed six financial crimes that could earn him twenty-eight years in prison. Milken agreed to a plea bargain in which he would pay "a $200 million fine and $400 million in a restitution fund for investors hurt by his crimes." Securities and Exchange chairman Richard Breeden said that Milken should do time because his guilty plea "demonstrates that he stood at the center of a network of deception, fraud and deceit."[15] Indeed, Milken had been indicted in September 1988, on ninety-eight racketeering counts filed in a 184-page document alleging the most sweeping violations ever perpetrated against the securities laws. Milken, the indictment charged, had "traded on inside information, manipulated stock prices, filed false disclosure forms with the Securities and Exchange Commission (SEC) in order to disguise stock ownership, filed fraudulent offering materials, kept false books and records, and defrauded [his] own clients." Milken, the god who ruled Wall Street for a whole decade, was now shown to be a supreme economic wilder, in fact, the biggest financial criminal in history.[16]

Milken, it turned out, had for years been running the country's entire junk bond market like a Mafia don. It was hard to tell whether his associates and clients were talking about Michael Milken or the other Michael, Mafia head Michael Corleone, made famous by Al Pacino in the movie, *The Godfather*. A Milken intimate says, "In addition to being a talented, creative genius, Michael is among the most avaricious, ruthless, venal people on the face of the earth." Another says, "Michael is interested in power, dominance, one hundred percent market share. Nothing is good enough for Michael. He is the most unhappy person I know. He never has enough." Like Corleone, Milken stopped at nothing to get control. Even after his indictment in 1988 he succeeded in getting exclusive control of the junk bond offerings of the biggest deals in the country, among them the RJR Nabisco takeover. A close member of Milken's group said Mike's nickname was "the Shep," referring to the brilliant, eccentric Corsican shepherd boy in Robert Ludlum's thriller, *The Matarese Circle*, who, obsessed by the need for control, masterminded a worldwide terrorist revolution through his control of global multinational corporations.[17]

Connie Bruck concluded after extensive interviews on Wall Street that "there are parallels between traditional organized crime and the organization that the patriarchal Milken built . . . the brass-knuckles, threatening, market-manipulating Cosa Nostra of the securities world." Milken did whatever was necessary (short of physical violence) to get a client and keep a client, ending up with the world's most powerful corporations and investment banks in his stable, even though he was gouging all his powerhouse clients regularly and many knew it. One of Milken's favorite sayings was, "If we can't make money off our friends, who can we make money off of?" Milken did not favor either buyers or sellers of junk; he took both under his wing and found, as described in the SEC indictments, exquisite ways to extort money from them, whether taking exorbitant commissions, demanding "warrants," a type of financial sweetener for the deal-maker, or distorting the price of the offerings, often by ingenious schemes involving unethical if not illegal buy-backs and trading on the extraordinary inside information available to him.[18]

Milken, virtually omnipotent, saw himself as outside both moral and legal constraints, regarding them as "mere conventions . . . for the foot soldiers of the world—the less creative, less aggressive, less visionary." Bruck writes that the King would make his own laws: "For whether it meant procuring women, or threatening would-be clients, the resounding credo at Drexel was to do whatever it took to win." At the nerve center of the American economy, Milken had created a veritable wilding machine. One Drexel associate said Mike's people "were animals, threatening companies." Another former Drexel executive was equally blunt, "It was all true, the place is a total slimebucket."[19]

Milken helped spawn a wilding culture, a kind of ethical jungle, throughout the business world that went well beyond criminal activities per se. Its trademark was its lust for quick money of dizzying amounts. In 1985, Drexel paid the King a cool $40 million bonus, while his overall income for 1987 was at least as high as $550 million, inspiring none other than David Rockefeller to remark that "such an extraordinary income inevitably raises questions as to whether there isn't something unbalanced in the way our financial system is working." In 1986, Milken's group at Drexel received over $250 million in bonuses. One of his associates, who got a $9 million cut, said "This is Disneyworld for adults."[20]

Milken's company rocketed to the fastest fortune ever made on Wall Street. In 1977, Drexel's revenues were about $150 million, but by 1985, it was making $2.5 billion in revenues, and in 1986, it pulled down a record $4 billion. In 1990, Drexel filed for Chapter Eleven bankruptcy, but that did not stop every company in America from gaping at Drexel's performance and fantasizing its own strategies for the fast buck.[21]

The romance with paper entrepreneurship still mesmerizes American business, despite the fall of Drexel and Milken and the re-regulation of the most nakedly criminal practices. The events at Drexel constitute a collective business wilding against society itself, partly because it unleashed a whole culture of Milken clones. One was Ivan Boesky, perhaps Wall Street's most publicized 1980s criminal, who confessed to insider trading after making hundreds of millions on takeover deals. Boesky solemnly stated the credo of his decade when he told a Berkeley commencement gathering, "Greed is healthy. You can be greedy and still feel good about yourself." Another Milken clone, Charlie Atkins, by age twenty-seven controlled a securities market worth $21 billion, but in 1987 was convicted of creating the largest tax shelter fraud in history. Found guilty on thirty-one charges of "bogus security transactions," Atkins faked tax losses running into the billions, with clients eventually suing him to recover over $2.5 billion. And there was the Billionaire Boys' Club, comprising a number of over-zealous yuppies, smitten with the new entrepreneurial fever, who were prepared to murder for a quick fortune. Joe Hunt, club leader, was convicted on April 22, 1987, for an eerie revenge killing to make up for a bad business deal.[22] The hope that the criminal side of Wall Street might be fading in the 1990s has been disproved by events catalogued in the next chapter, including the late-1991 revelation that Salomon Brothers, one of Wall Street's three largest and most prestigious trading firms, faced possible disbarment as a trader in government securities after admitting serious and extensive illegal operations.

But beyond such overt criminal wilding is a more insidious wilding of businesses making huge pots of money without making anything useful. Corrupting in any era, its economic and moral consequences are staggering in the current period. Multiply manyfold the $6.2 billion that Henry Kravis was paying to buy Beatrice Companies, the $6 billion that Samuel Heyman was paying to take over Union Carbide, the $25 billion that Milken helped raise to pay for RJR Nabisco, and one gets a quick idea of the volume of capital — and mountain of debt — that were going, not to reequip the American economy to compete with the Japanese and Germans, but rather to enrich America's corporate elite. Paper entrepreneurship has become institutionalized wilding on a gargantuan scale, diverting America's capital resources away from its areas of true need: education, housing, transportation, job creation, the environment, and the poor.

Among the legacies of such promiscuous wilding: the ballooning of the deficit, the milking of the federal treasury, the worsening of the Savings and Loan crisis, and ultimately the undermining of America's international competitiveness as well as the fabric of American society itself. "The main story is the cost of these [paper] deals to society at large," Michael Thomas wrote in the *New York Review of Books*. "Junk financing is a fraud," he explains, because it allows the interest on the debt to be deducted, thus bleeding the federal treasury, "even though no penny actually changes hands." And, Thomas adds, "We know that huge junk-bond investments figured in the more outrageous debacles in the Savings and Loan crisis," as well as in a looming pension fund emergency growing out of the use of pension funds to finance takeovers. "We taxpayers might well start taking for granted the likelihood that once we have finished paying the bills for the S and L crisis, we may be called upon to pay the bills for a crisis in pension funds."[23]

Robert Reich, who coined the term "paper entrepreneurship," puts the ultimate cost succinctly: "It has hastened our collective decline."[24]

The Not-So-Invisible Hand in the White House Cookie Jar: Wilding in Washington

Business people were not the only leaders who caught Reagan's entrepreneurial fever and propagated the wilding bug. So did politicians, including those at the highest levels. More than 240 high-level Reagan appointees eventually became targets of investigation for ethical or criminal wrongdoing. These political entrepreneurs made their own contribution to rewriting the American Dream, instructing millions of already cynical Americans that every vocation, including public service, was now fair game for entrepreneurs looking for a fast buck.

When the Reagans came to Washington, Nancy Reagan told the *Washington Post* that she and her husband planned to "set an example for a return to a higher sense of morality" when they moved into the White House. "It kind of filters down from the top," she said. During the 1988 presidential campaign, Democratic candidate Michael Dukakis offered a somewhat different interpretation of what had "filtered down" when he observed that "a fish rots from the head first."[25]

Pennsylvania Avenue began to rival Wall Street itself as a venue of outrageous wilding. As with the S and L banks after deregulation, entrepreneurial cowboys took over virtually every government agency: Housing and Urban Development, Defense, Interior, Commerce, even Justice, and turned them into veritable cash cows for their own purposes. But unlike the S and L entrepreneurs, these were top government appointees practicing a kind of political paper entrepreneurship, raiding the public treasury without returning anything of value. And the closer they were to Ronald Reagan himself, the more flagrant the wilding.

Consider Edwin Meese, perhaps Reagan's closest advisor, who became attorney general: the national symbol of morality and chief enforcer of justice. Reagan, who had worked with Meese for years in California, said that he always knew him "to be a man of honesty and integrity," indeed had never caused him "a moment's embarrassment" — a curious comment since Meese earned the dubious distinction of becoming the first man to be investigated by three special prosecutors. There was hardly a day in which Meese and the general public did not wake to face headlines like that in the *New York Times* on July

22, 1988 "Wedtech Prosecutor Assails Meese As 'A Sleaze.'"
Sleaze was the image that clung to the affable attorney general,
based on the endless revelations about his generosity to people
who did favors for him. Meese secured the appointment of Edwin Thomas to the U.S. Postal Service Board of Governors after Thomas arranged $60,000 in loans for him. Meese also
greased the appointment of the man who made a $15,000 loan
to his wife, Ursula, to head the San Fransisco General Services
Administration.[26]

The Office of Government Ethics found Meese in violation
of federal ethical standards, as did several Congressional committees and independent special prosecutors. Independent
Counsel James McKay concluded after a lengthy investigation
that Ed Meese "probably violated the criminal law" four times
after he became attorney general, by filing false income taxes,
failing to pay capital gains taxes on time, and intervening on
matters in which he had a direct financial stake. In other words,
Meese approached his service as attorney general in the entrepreneurial spirit of his era, sinking the Justice Department
itself into a virtually unparalleled swamp of unethical activities, and making it a travesty of the criminal groups it was supposed to investigate. One of his former colleagues, Arnold
Burns, told the Senate Judiciary Committee that Meese turned
the Justice Department into "a world of Alice in Wonderland,"
where "up was down and down was up, in was out and out was
in, happy was sad and sad was happy, rain was sunshine and
sunshine was rain, and hot was cold and cold was hot." Honest
lawyers, including Burns and William Weld, quit the department in droves.[27]

Major government departments all over Washington became wilding machines. The Department of Defense (DOD),
for example, began to resemble Drexel Burnham, a fantasy
come true for an army of fortune seekers. Defense contracts
became as profitable as junk bonds, institutionalized channels
for officials, clients, and middlemen to rip off billions. Lewis
Lapham observes that "bills of criminal particulars could be ex-

tended to almost the entire list of clients doing business with the Pentagon," and indeed by 1985 criminal investigations had already been launched against forty-five of the hundred largest defense contractors. Making it all possible were DOD appointees at the top, such as Deputy Defense Secretary Paul Thayer, who in 1984 resigned amidst charges of insider trading and ended up serving nineteen months for perjury and obstruction of justice.[28]

Housing and Urban Development (HUD) was also crawling with paper entrepreneurs, under the permissive management of Secretary Samuel Pierce. Deputy Assistant Secretary DuBois Gilliam testified bluntly how they did business: "We dealt strictly in politics." In other words, HUD only doled out its money for clients who returned the favor, people who directly paid off HUD's entrepreneurial employees, or had connections with bigwigs who could pull strings in HUD. Gilliam gave revealing clues about how Secretary Pierce ran HUD. Before he left the department, Gilliam figured he deserved more than the $100,000 in bribes he had already taken, so he went to Pierce's office and asked for a farewell gift of 400 units worth of housing renovation subsidies. Pierce's aide "came back and told me I had 250 units," worth only $2 million. "I couldn't have the 400 units," Gilliam said, "because I was being greedy." Gilliam served an eighteen-month term in prison for taking bribes, while a special prosecutor investigated Secretary Pierce on charges of steering money to clients of his former law firm, influence peddling, bribery, perjury, and conspiracy to defraud the government.[29]

Meanwhile, investigators had already had a field day over at the Department of Interior, first with Secretary James Watts, and then with his Environmental Protection Agency (EPA) chief Anne Gorsuch (later Anne Burford), who was forced to resign after reports of "sweetheart" settlements in the Toxic Waste Program and subsequent allegations of perjury, conflict of interest, and destruction of subpoenaed documents. Burford had conveniently purchased two shredders for the agency, perhaps with money saved by reducing by almost two-thirds the number of environmental cases they referred for prosecution. At least six Congressional committees investigated the trail of EPA's paper entrepreneurs, leading to Burford's ouster, but only after President Reagan, typically supportive of his political entrepreneurs caught with their hands in the jar, told her that she could leave with her "head held high." He blamed her problems on "environmental extremists," who would not be happy "until the White House looks like a bird's nest."[30]

Elsewhere, at the Department of Commerce, Deputy Secretary Guy W. Fiske had to resign after the public learned he was interviewing for a job as president of a satellite communications company while making decisions about selling government weather satellites to private industry. At the Labor Department, Secretary Raymond Donovan also had to resign after being indicted on fraud and larceny. Veterans Administration chief Robert P. Nimmo resigned after the public learned that he spent over $50,000 in government funds to redecorate his office. National Security Advisor Richard Allen resigned after accepting money from a Japanese magazine. (Allen protested: "I didn't accept it. I received it.") Later, Deputy National Security Advisor Thomas C. Reed resigned after journalists reported that he traded on inside information to turn a $427,000 profit on a $3,125 investment.[31]

Michael Deaver, one of the president's closest advisors, emerged as the country's most public political entrepreneur, openly trading on his connection to the president and bragging to journalists that he was "making far more than I ever thought I would." Even before he left the White House, Deaver was reported to have lined up clients for his new lobbying firm, including the governments of Canada, South Korea, and Puerto Rico. Deaver surfaced on *Time* magazine's cover in a black Jaguar, leading even Nancy Reagan, not shy about flaunting wealth, to tell her friend Deaver, "You made a big mistake." Deaver was later convicted of three counts of perjury, getting a suspended three-year sentence, 1,500 hours of community service, and a $100,000 fine. "It was a very fair sentence," Deaver told reporters, "if I had been guilty."[32]

Nixon's aides, convicted of Watergate criminality, confessed their sins, but Reagan's men never experienced a pang of remorse, testimony to the grip of the new wilding culture. Neither Deaver, nor Meese, nor any of the other wilders in the Reagan administration, ever saw themselves as anything but victims of political harassment, having lost the ability to distinguish between crime and public service. Being on the take is an honored principle of American politics, but it became standard operational procedure in the Reagan White House. The paper entrepreneurs in Reagan's cabinet were so imbued with the new entrepreneurial ideology of their boss that they redefined greed as initiative, theft as capitalizing on opportunity.

4

Bushwhacked!
Washington and Wall Street
Go Wild: II

It is necessary that the prince should know how to
color his nature well, and to be a great hypocrite and
dissembler.

MACHIAVELLI

RONALD REAGAN, like Franklin Delano Roosevelt, is that
rare President appearing every generation or so who
pushes society in a radical new direction. The influence of such
leaders outlives their presidencies, for the presidents who follow them are mostly mopper-uppers, fleshing out their
predecessors' new paradigm. President Bush became an unex-
pectedly skilled salesman of the Reagan Dream, giving the new
wilding culture a human face.

President Bush seemed to be taking the country on a new
course, when he talked of a "kinder, gentler America." In fact,
during the 1988 campaign, Bush derided "this fast-buck stuff
. . . I don't have great respect for just going out and stacking
up money." In his inaugural address, Bush said: "In our hearts,
we know what matters. We cannot only hope to leave our children a bigger car, a bigger bank account." Speech-writer Peggy
Noonan wrote that the words Bush most prized were love, family, and children.

In his 1988 campaign, he declared himself the education
president, the environment president, the compassion president, a man of values, not money. Bush had pronounced at
his inauguration that Americans did not simply want to be

known as people who "were more driven to succeed than any-one around us." Two years into his term, in 1990, the fall of Donald Trump and Michael Milken seemed to reinforce the notion that Bush was helping to end the age of economic wild-ing. In May 1989, the *Wall Street Journal* reported, "The message is clear: Rich is out."

But if Bush dramatically shifted the tone and style of the presidency, it may have only been to defend the basic thrust of the Reagan Revolution. "Bush represented a shift from the aggressiveness of the new rich," Kevin Phillips writes, "to the defensiveness, even social conciliation of established wealth." Bush represents "old wealth"—an elite of "trust funds, third-generation summer cottages on Fisher's Island, and grand-fathers with Dillon Read or Brown Brothers Harriman"—which seeks to govern capitalism in a decorous, restrained manner. The spectacle of "hogs feeding at the trough," David Stockman's way of characterizing the excesses of the Reagan administration, could create a public backlash, one that blue-blooded Republicans like George Herbert Walker Bush had historically sought to avert.[1]

In 1980, Bush called Reagan's program "voodoo economics," and he was said to be personally embarrassed by the Reagan circle's shameless flaunting of wealth. But as loyal vice president, he assumed the mantle of leading cheerleader for Reaga-nomics, prompting former Carter Press Secretary Jody Powell to comment: "It's not the fetching and heeling but the excessive tail-wagging that grates." But Bush was genuinely smitten with the magic of the market and the mystique of the entrepreneur. "Let individuals have as much leeway and flexibility as possi-ble . . . as free a market as possible," Bush preached in 1988. He unleashed a series of economic policy initiatives to preserve into the twenty-first century the essentials of Reaganomics. Bush's "Read My Lips. No new taxes." pose is widely credited with encouraging a "may the public be damned, I'll take mine" attitude, close to the heart of the new wilding culture. More-over, while he eventually changed course and agreed to tax revenue increases, his commitment to further liberating the entrepreneur by slashing capital gains taxes never wavered. Nor did his commitment to preserving the broader tax revolution of the Reagan years, which had eroded the progressivity of income taxes and massively redistributed income to the rich.

Meanwhile, Bush, despite his rhetoric of compassion, perpetuated a policy of "benign neglect" to the low- and middle-income groups that were picking up the rich's tax tab. His annual budgets offered slim pickings for the homeless, the poor, the uneducated, the medically uninsured, battered wives, abused children, and the millions of working families struggling harder to pay the bills and send the kids to school. Pulling the public plug on the mushrooming population of the needy and disregarding the vast menu of social problems were the most virulent forms of Reaganite public policy wilding, a wilding that Bush embraced, lending it respectability by cloaking it in the sparkling rhetoric of "a thousand points of light."[2]

On deregulation, too, the key policy that unleashed paper entrepreneurialism, Bush has been militant, living up to his campaign promise to "kick a little butt." He nominated Richard Breeden as chairman of the Securities and Exchange Commission, a man who espoused further deregulation of Wall Street and vehemently opposed any restraints on the corporate "urge to merge." Wall Street read the Bush signals with enthusiasm, plunging back into speculations that by 1990 were pushing the Dow Jones above an unprecedented 3000 mark. The pace of takeovers only slightly abated in early 1990, with huge new deals no longer raising eyebrows or gleaning headlines. By mid-1991, "highly irrational, destabilizing speculative forces" had become so entrenched, writes Wall Street watcher Eamonn Fingleton, that they not only posed the risk of another Black Monday crash, but were forcing "corporate managers to think increasingly short-term in a world marketplace where long-term thinking has never been more important."[3] Wall Street entrepreneurs were joined by entrepreneurial colleagues in art auctions and rare coin purchases setting records of their own. "In domestic economics, despite new rhetoric," Kevin Phillips concludes, "the essential policies of the Reagan years continued . . . the commitment to market economics, the free flow of capital and the uninhibited commitment to accumulation of wealth" had become virtual dogma in the Bush era.[4]

Nowhere is the thread tying Bush to Reagan more evident than in the Savings and Loan crisis, the biggest orgy of economic wilding in history. The S and L crisis is paper entrepreneurialism run fantastically amuk, bred from the pell-mell deregulation of Reaganomics. Deregulation brought out of the woodwork two breeds of wilding entrepreneurs, the first a loosely coordinated band of Mafia style outlaws, "mobsters, arms dealers, drug-money launderers and the most unlikely cast of wheeler dealers that ever prowled the halls of financial institutions." S and L researchers Stephen Pizzo, Mary Fricker, and Paul Muola describe this group, which took over hundreds of banks, as a "network that was sucking millions of dollars from thrifts through a purposeful and coordinated system of fraud." William Seidman, chairman of the Resolution Trust Corporation, the agency set up to rescue the thrifts, confirmed that "criminal fraud was discovered in 60 percent of the savings institutions seized by the government in 1989." FBI director William Sessions said in testimony before the House Banking Committee that criminal fraud was so "pervasive" that it "is truly a national crisis." A second group of high-roller entrepreneurs who took over S and Ls stayed within the law but made absurdly risky investments in junk bonds and commercial real estate, as well as in high-risk car, mobile home, credit card, and consumer loans. These investments were made possible by the Reagan-Bush administration's deregulatory policy. The tab to the American people is likely to be $500 billion, an astounding cost to every American household of more than $5,000.[5]

During Reagan's tenure, Edwin Gray, head of the Federal Home Loan Bank, complained that the "White House was full

of ideologues, particularly free market types," who were rabid-
ly stoking the S and L crisis by their mania for deregulation.
The way to solve the problem, they said, was more deregulation, which meant not only legalizing and underwriting outra-
geously speculative investments and loans but funding fewer
examiners. Gray complained that he was "repeatedly turned
down in his bids for more inspectors to police, or shut down,
the freewheeling thrifts created by deregulation."[6] The silver
lining of the S and L crisis is that it has made perfectly transpar-
ent the connection between economic policy and economic
wilding.

Although Bush did not create the initial S and L problem,
he is complicitous in major ways, beyond the fact that he willingly signed on to the banking deregulatory package as vice
president. The public symbol of the Bush connection is his son,
Neil Bush, who in 1990 was charged by the U.S. Office of Thrift
Supervision with flagrant conflict-of-interest for approving
huge loans to his business partners, including more than $100
million to Bill Walters, his business partner and later his credi-
tor, when Bush was a director of the Silverado S and L in Denver. Bush also faced more serious charges for conspiring with
other Silverado directors to require borrowers to "kick back
about 20 percent of their loans to buy largely worthless stock
in the S and L," which eventually collapsed in 1988 at a cost
of one billion dollars to the taxpayers. Bert Ely, a respected S
and L analyst, said "Neil Bush has criminal exposure there the
same way other directors have." The U.S. government $200
million dollar suit against Neil Bush and his codirectors was
settled out of court in 1991, with Bush and his fellow defendants
agreeing to pay the Federal Deposit Insurance Corporation
(FDIC) $26.5 million. President Bush defended his son as a
"good kid," and, indeed, Neil followed in his father's footsteps
by launching his career as an entrepreneur in the oil business,
before he "hooked up with a crowd of high rollers" who brought
him into the fast money of the S and L business.[7]

The political organization Common Cause reports a more

immediate connection between President Bush and the S and Ls: the fact that Bush received more than $600,000 in his 1988 presidential campaign from S and L executives. There is evidence of direct connections between Bush aides, such as Robert J. Thompson, a former Bush Congressional liaison, and S and L entrepreneurs, like James M. Fail, previously indicted for fraud, who was permitted, in December 1988, to purchase fifteen failed S and L banks. Thompson apparently interceded for Fail with the Dallas Federal Home Loan Bank board that approved the deal, leading to charges of political favoritism and sweetheart deals that might reach up to President Bush.[8]

In mid-1990, questions developed about whether President Bush had, in fact, created a second S and L crisis by dragging his feet on the prosecution of S and L criminals while helping to transfer the financial cost from the wilders to the public. Senator Howard Metzenbaum, investigating S and L fraud, claimed that the American people are "sick of stories about fast-living buccaneers who first escaped with their money and who are now escaping prosecution." In March 1990, *Time* magazine lambasted Bush for letting at least 1,500 of 3,500 major S and L criminal cases "gather dust," claiming that "the dire shortage of sleuths is partly caused by the Bush administration's unwillingness to lay out a measly $25 million" — in a $500 billion crisis. Critics also charge that Bush engaged in a massive unloading of failed S and Ls to the very entrepreneurial crowd responsible for the crisis, as in the case of Fail, who was permitted to buy his S and Ls with only $1,000 of his own money, while being promised $1.8 billion in federal subsidies. William Greider minces no words in accusing the Bush administration of looking at the "S and L crisis as a fire sale — an opportunity for private investors to pick over the carcasses," buying for a steal and getting out with huge profits. "Big league investors and major Wall Street firms," Greider writes, "are circling around the bailout process, buying choice carcasses at concessionary prices." He maintains this is only the beginning of the "fire sale" that "promises to be a long and costly debacle for the American taxpayers."[9]

Meanwhile, in mid-1991, Greider sounded the alarm on a wilding crisis spreading through the wider commercial banking industry, charging that the Bush administration intends to conceal it behind a "veil of silence" until after the 1992 elections. The "second bank robbery," as Greider put it in the *New York Times*, is a "monstrous scandal" that may plague Americans through much of the 1990s. At stake is the survival of some of the most famous banks in America, including Citibank, Chase Manhattan, Manufacturers Hanover, Chemical, First Chicago, and Security Pacific. [10]

The dimensions of the new crisis are sobering. Comptroller General Charles Bowsher told a Senate panel in September 1990, that the FDIC, which insures bank depositors for up to $100,000 per account, was almost broke. By 1991, with the recession in full force and the FDIC list of "problem" banks rapidly expanding, the FDIC was expected to go $32 billion into debt. The *New York Times* reported that "bank losses are the worst in fifty years," with a "big rise" in the number and average size of failures: 1,048 banks with $408.8 billion in assets, representing 12.1 percent of the industry total, were at serious risk. In early 1991, the FDIC forecast 440 failures in 1991 and 1992, with the most catastrophic possibility being collapse of the "big boys" such as Citibank or Chase Manhattan.[11]

Like S and L entrepreneurs, many bank executives threw traditional banking restraint to the wind, greedily overinvesting in shopping centers, office buildings, and other seductive speculations that have gone sour in the 1990s. The FDIC reported that "the real estate problems of the Northeast have spread to the mid-Atlantic states, and signs of real estate weakness have appeared in several southeastern states." *Los Angeles Times* reporter Robert A. Rosenblatt wrote that the Savings and Loan nightmare "is back again in a new form" and Alabama senator Richard T. Shelton worried that "If the sky is not falling, it is shaky."[12]

As of mid-1991, Bush was mainly concerned about the impact on his own reelection. In 1987, the Reagan administration papered over the S and L crisis, "so they could get through the 1988 elections without bothering the folks back home. The Bush regime is following the same script."[13] But the Bush administration's involvement goes beyond cover-up efforts; as with the S and Ls, Bush is trying to bail out the banks at the expense of the public. Congressman Henry Gonzalez, the chairman of the House Banking Committee says that a get-tough approach is essential to protect the public from the costs of another huge bailout. Gonzalez urged in 1991 that rather than coddling the banks at risk, the "government should shut Citibank right now." But while one-third of Citibank's $13.3 billion real estate loans in 1991 were "nonperforming," the Bush regulators blew Citibank "a kiss — a required writedown of only $400 million" in contrast to the two or three billion dollars anticipated by the financial markets. Bush regulators were "propping up the troubled banks with lenient accounting and hidden subsidies, and hoping for the best."[14]

Instead of imposing a tougher regulatory discipline on the banks, Bush's solution "is more deregulation — administration proposals that would let banks cross state lines and get into other lines of business." This is precisely the strategy that burned the public in the S and L crisis. Greider notes that the Democrats are wary of further deregulation in the light of the S and L experience, but, like the Republicans, hope "that the public doesn't get interested. When the big money gets in trouble, Washington runs away from the facts."[15]

Foot-dragging and a possible cover-up emerged as well in the notorious scandal of the Bank of Credit and Commerce International (BCCI). The scale of BCCI wilding, involving global money-laundering and drug-running, dwarfs that of any other bank in history. While BCCI is an international bank operating in over seventy-seven countries, the crisis has touched numerous prominent Americans, including Clark Clifford, advisor to five U.S. presidents. Clifford represented

BCCI in its efforts to operate and buy banks in the United States and chaired First American, a secret BCCI subsidiary. The question of Bush administration involvement has been raised by many critics, including Senate investigator Jack Blum, who got on BCCI's trail as early as 1988 during the Senate's investigation of former Panamanian leader Manuel Noriega. By 1989, Blum had so much information about BCCI "irregularities," including illicit drug financing, bribery, and deceptive accounting to cover up the complete collapse of its assets, that he repeatedly contacted the Justice Department. The department stonewalled Blum, saying they would contact him when necessary, while holding up, as the *New York Times* reported in 1991, any serious investigation. Only after Blum finally took his information to Robert M. Morgenthau, the district attorney in Manhattan, did American prosecutors begin seriously to go after BCCI. As of late 1991, the reasons for the Bush administration's inaction remain murky, with speculations ranging from sheer bureaucratic bungling to a cover-up to shield prominent government officials or prevent revelations about other administration embarrassments, such as the Noriega case or the Iran-Contra affair.[16]

The public is also being kept in the dark about a looming wilding crisis in the insurance industry, with frightening parallels to the S and L and commerical bank crises. While no one predicts wholesale collapse, insurance companies are presently failing at seven times the rate of ten years ago. In the first eight months of 1991, regulators seized three huge insurance companies in hazardous financial condition: Executive Life, First Capital Life, and Mutual Benefit Life. In Rhode Island, the private deposit insurance system for protecting customers of failed insurance companies has already collapsed.[17]

The story of California's Executive Life, with 208,000 life insurance policyholders and 164,000 annuity holders throughout the country, reveals some of the wilding dimensions of the crisis. Regulators seized the company in April 1991, after customers scurried to cash in their policies, alarmed by news of the company's perilous financial situation. The *New York Times* reported that Executive Life "had gambled more of its money on junk bonds than any other large insurer." When many of these defaulted, the company's balance sheet was jeopardized.[18]

Much like the banks, many insurance companies abandoned their traditional prudence in the 1980s and speculated in risky real estate investments as well as in junk bonds. Executive Life's chief executive was Fred Carr, a former Wall Street money manager associated with Michael Milken. Carr reshaped the staid insurance company in the spirit of high-rolling Drexel Burnham. Carr's policies led not only to an investigation by the California Insurance Commission into the propriety of undisclosed company practices, but brought the company to the brink of liquidation and disaster for thousands of policyholders, averted only when two French investing houses offered to buy Executive Life. Michael Morrissey, chairman of the Firemark Group, an insurance research firm, acknowledged that such developments had given the insurance business "more bad press" than any time in the over twenty years he has been in the business.[19]

President Bush, of course, cannot be blamed for the greed or recklessness of insurance executives. The responsibility for the wilding crises in both banking and insurance falls mainly on the offending entrepreneurs. But Bush's deregulatory policies created the context that encouraged lax supervision, indulgent rating standards, and more speculative investment options.

Iran-Contra and the October Surprise

Turning from domestic to foreign policy concerns, Bush's role in the Iran-Contra scandal, the central foreign policy wilding caper of the Reagan years, is so serious that it has periodically sparked speculation about potential impeachment, as well as persistent rumors of Quayle's appointment as "impeachment insurance." Here, we turn to a different form of political wilding involving alleged illegal and covert government policies, sometimes followed by illegal cover-ups. Such wilding is different from the corruption intended to enrich individual politicians or their business allies. It involves circumventing the law and deceiving the public to implement unpopular policies or to ensure political survival.

In 1991, the Iran-Contra scandal resurfaced when Bush nominated Robert Gates to be his new director of the CIA. In 1987, President Reagan had had to withdraw his own nomination of Gates as CIA director after Congress raised serious doubts as to whether Gates had told the truth about his knowledge of the illicit Contra funding. Regarding his own involvement, Bush has refused comment, beyond denying all knowledge about Iranian arms sales and diversion of profits, claiming to have been "out of the loop" and away at the Harvard-Yale football game during a crucial meeting. Despite Bush's denials, evidence continues to surface that Bush had knowledge about the covert war being waged out of Oliver North's White House basement office. When American CIA pilot Eugene Hasenfus was shot down over Nicaragua, he told the *Washington Post* that Bush was aware of his Contra operation. Felix Rodriguez, one of the CIA's chief operatives in the covert war, constantly telephoned Bush's office from his command post in El Salvador, reporting to Donald Gregg, Bush's foreign policy aide and a former CIA operative in Vietnam, where he served with Rodriguez. Polls indicate that a majority of Americans believe that Bush is lying about what he knew and when he knew it, a not unreasonable suspicion given Gregg's closeness to Bush.[20]

A potentially even more serious wilding scandal concerns the "October Surprise," described by *Los Angeles Times* reporter Doyle McManus as the "most diabolical intrigue of the century." Since the early 1980s, rumors have circulated regarding a "secret deal in 1980 between Ronald Reagan, George Bush, and Iran's Ayatollah Khomeini to keep fifty-two American hostages imprisoned in Tehran until that year's election day, thus sealing Reagan's march to the White House." While denied by President Bush's spokesman, Steve Hart, as "absolutely false—a pure fabrication," the story gained new credibility in April 1991, when Gary Sick, a Columbia University professor and former Carter administration National Security Council officer responsible for Iran and the 1980 hostage negotiations, wrote an article in the *New York Times* (and, later, a book) about his own research on the subject. Based on hundreds of interviews with American and Iranian government officials and military personnel, Sick concludes, "The weight of testimony has overcome my initial doubts." Specifically, Sick reports that he is now convinced that several meetings did take place between Reagan campaign officials and Iranian intermediaries about the timing of the hostage release, including two key meetings in July 1980 between William Casey, the Reagan-Bush campaign chair, and Mehdi Karrudi, an important Iranian cleric. Karrudi promised to "cooperate with the Reagan campaign about the timing of any hostage release," Sick writes, in return for assistance in unfreezing Iranian assets and in acquiring desperately needed arms.[21]

Sick also describes a second series of meetings in Paris from October 15 to October 20 in which the deal was purportedly sealed. Sick claims that at least "five of the sources who say they were in Paris in connection with these meetings insist that George Bush was present for at least one meeting. Three of the sources say that they saw him there."[22] In his denials, which, interestingly, have been limited to denials of his own personal involvement rather than of the secret deal itself, Bush has had to account for his disappearance from public view from 9:00 PM, October 18 to 7:00 PM, October 19. As of mid-1991, his alibis were unconvincing since they were contradictory. Two Secret Service agents testified that Bush was at the Chevy Chase Country Club in suburban Maryland on private business; Vice President Quayle said that Bush had spent all day at home without a Secret Service escort; the Secret Service has told the *Wall Street Journal* that Bush was actually lunching with Supreme Court Justice Potter Stewart and his wife. Unfortunately, this last cannot be confirmed since Stewart is now dead and his wife has chronic memory loss. Nonetheless, the evidence of the president's involvement or knowledge remains purely circumstantial.[23]

President Bush's problems were enhanced in June 1991, when Ronald Reagan himself hinted that the story was true. When asked whether there had been any preelection contacts with the Iranian government in 1980 about the timing of the hostage release, Reagan astonished reporters by saying, "Not by me," implying, as the *Boston Globe* noted, "that he knew — and wanted the world to know — that other members of his campaign had conducted private negotiations with the Khomeini regime." When reporters asked if he meant that campaign officials were, indeed, involved, Reagan replied, "I can't get into details. Some of these things are still classified." As the *Globe* noted, "The scandalous truth about any such contacts would be that they were not governmental; hence they could not be classified." The Great Communicator was finding his own way to tell the public part of the story without letting the politically explosive details leak out.[24]

New York Times columnist Leslie Gelb wrote that as of mid-1991 "there is now strong circumstantial evidence" the secret deal did take place, a conclusion also reached by a team of independent investigators for the Public Broadcast System's documentary series "Frontline." Gelb joined Sick and a group of the 1980 Iranian hostages in insisting on an official investigation, noting that, if true, the story is "so subversive of the democratic process and presidential authority" that it constitutes "treachery." Indeed, if true, it is political wilding of the highest order, involving not only a willingness by Bush and other American leaders to undermine national elections, but also to play with the lives of hostages, lie to the people, and tamper with foreign policy for purely partisan benefits, while also exposing American leaders to the horrendous prospect of future blackmailing by the Iranian leadership. In July 1991, Congress launched its own formal investigation from which to reach its own conclusions.[25]

Part of Bush's legacy may be a culture of political wilding, in which a president not only deceives the public with the practiced discipline of a CIA director, but exploits visual symbolism and thirty-second sound bites with unprecedented cynicism. Bush's 1988 campaign was an orgy of negative campaigning, evoking racial bigotry with the Willie Horton ad campaign and pandering to national chauvinism with nonstop visits to flag factories. Journalist Elizabeth Drew, in her book on the 1988 election, writes, "The Bush campaign broke the mold of modern presidential politics. Negative campaigning of a new order of magnitude has now come to presidential politics." Drew concludes: "A degradation occurred which we may have to live with for a long time." In 1990, when Bush broke his "Read My Lips. No new taxes." pledge, the central commitment of his campaign, the public level of cynicism was already so high that little surprise was registered, people no longer expecting their president to say what he means or to say anything other than what is opportune at the moment. In contrast, twenty years earlier, public shock about the Watergate caper, a trivial "dirty trick" compared to either the Iran-Contra or October Surprise allegations, forced President Nixon out of office.[26]

Bushwhacking in the Gulf: A Case of Global Wilding?

President Bush will be remembered in history books primarily for his conduct of the Gulf war. Bush faced serious aggression and proved skillful and steady in bringing the world community together. But sober historical analysis may reveal the Gulf war as "global wilding" — savage violence to advance the "national interest," accompanied by massive indifference to the plight of the victims.

What national interest drove Bush to war? Bob Woodward offers evidence that, despite all the rhetoric about democracy and a new world order, this was a war, in substantial measure, about oil prices. In the administration's first strategy meeting after Saddam Hussein's troops rolled over Kuwait, Bush launched into a detailed discussion of oil prices, asserting that Saddam, with only one-fifth of the world's supply, could manipulate pricing and hold the entire Western world hostage. Defense Secretary Richard Cheney argued that Saddam's control of "20 percent of the world's oil presents a significant threat," and National Security Advisor Brent Scowcroft said that Iraq's new oil wealth made it a dangerous new superpower rival; all the top Bush advisors were fixated on the geopolitics of oil. There was no discussion of human rights or international law when the administration decided to go to war. This confirms the view voiced at peace rallies that despite the lofty rhetoric of the president, if the Middle East had been a broccoli field rather than an oil field, the United States would have stayed home.[27]

When Bush said publicly that this was a war "to defend the American way of life," he was confirming that the United States was prepared to do whatever necessary to ensure that Americans could pump gas into their tanks at a reasonable price. Blood for oil is, indeed, collective wilding to ensure the promise of the American Dream. Such global wilding by American presidents and other world leaders is not new, arising time and again from the lawlessness of the international system as well as the imperial ambitions of nations addicted to wealth and power. But as murderous, self-interested violence uninhibited by any feeling for the victims it has some uncanny parallels with the wilding disorder that consumed Charles Stuart, played out in a radically different form on the grand stage of world politics. Such a comparison does not assume personal malice on the part of the president, nor obviously any resemblance between Bush and Stuart in their private lives, since Mr. Bush appears to be a humane man in his personal affairs and enjoys a successful family life. But the president invoked mass violence—when other alternatives were available and were supported by some of his top military advisors—to advance American economic interests. Stuart would use any means necessary to get his restaurant; Bush resorted to war, the most extreme policy available to a president, partly to ensure that the prices in the collective American restaurant would not be determined by a tin-pot dictator. Stuart showed no restraint and no remorse, nor, we shall see, did the president.[28]

Oil was not the only or even the most important wilding motive, as Americans learned after the war when Bush exulted in a meeting with Congressmen, "By God, we've kicked the Vietnam syndrome, once and for all." American wars typically have vital symbolic as well as economic purposes, and, as Noam Chomsky put it starkly, this war sent an unambiguous message not only to Saddam Hussein but to all other Third World leaders that might cross the United States: "What we say goes. We are the masters, you shine our shoes and don't ever forget it." Bush himself put the point more gently, suggesting that the United States "has a new credibility." The new world order would still be ruled by force, an American force no longer hamstrung by Soviet counterbalance.[29]

The image of global wilding is reinforced by the accumulating evidence that Bush *wanted* war—or at minimum failed to pursue many possible peace options. *Newsday* journalist Knut Royce reported that in August, a week after the invasion of Kuwait, Saddam offered to withdraw in exchange for two tiny islands providing Gulf access (according to Chomsky, "uninhabited mudflats assigned to Kuwait in the imperial settlement, leaving Iraq landlocked") and control of the Ramallah oil field, 95 percent of which is inside Iraq. Iraqi Deputy Foreign Minister Nizar Hamdoon brought the offer to Washington on August 9, but it was summarily rejected by the National

Security Council on August 10; former CIA director Richard Helms thought it a serious offer and tried to revive it to no avail. Chomsky has documented a series of other rebuffed or unanswered initiatives, including a French initiative for Iraqi withdrawal from Kuwait "in exchange for a meaningless Security Council statement on a possible future conference," which both the United States and the United Kingdom announced they would veto. *New York Times* chief diplomatic correspondent Thomas Friedman reported that by mid-August, the United States had taken the position that the "diplomatic track" had to be blocked, since it could lead to token concessions such as "a Kuwaiti island or minor border adjustments" that might "defuse the crisis."[30]

A Catholic weekly close to the Vatican wrote that Bush deserves "the Nobel War Prize," since he "had the very concrete possibility of a just peace and he chose war," a point given yet further reinforcement by revelations that General Colin Powell, the country's top military leader, had favored continuation of sanctions as an alternative to war. Powell called it "strangulation," a policy also apparently favored by Secretary of State James Baker. Powell felt that the sanctions were preventing virtually all goods from getting into Iraq, and that sooner or later they were certain to work.

Indeed, the sanctions, reported by the CIA in December 1990 to have cut off 90 percent of Iraq's imports and 97 percent of its exports, may have actually worked very early on, leading to Saddam's peace offer of August 9. Powell felt that his message was not getting through to an entrenched president. Bush, however, did respond in October to General Powell, saying he felt there was no time politically for the sanctions approach; some have interpreted this as meaning that Bush was afraid that sticking with sanctions might drag the crisis into 1992, posing an unwelcome challenge to his reelection campaign. In any case, no further serious debate about the unadvisability of war took place inside the administration.[31]

When war came, it hit Iraq with the force Bush had

promised, no sissy war with "one hand tied behind our back" as the president likes to describe U.S. activities in Vietnam. The media has left the impression of a "clean" or "surgical" war, high-tech bombs guided by sci-fi delivery systems. TV inundated the public with images of laser bombs miraculously honing in on vital military targets while sparing civilians. But an uncharacteristic comment from CNN anchorman Bernard Shaw, who reported the war from Baghdad, told the true story: "Ladies and Gentlemen, I've never been there, but it feels like we're in the center of Hell."

The "clean" war proved to be, according to a March 1991 United Nations survey, "near apocalyptic." The report reads:

> Nothing that we had seen or read had quite prepared us for the particular form of devastation which has now wrought the country. . . . Now, most means of modern life support have been destroyed or rendered tenuous. Iraq has, for some time to come, been relegated to a preindustrial age.

Among the civilian casualties: the "total loss" of the civilian telecommunication system, crippling of the Iraqi electrical power grid and Iraq's network of roads and bridges, destruction of the country's sole laboratory producing veterinary vaccines as well as its "seed warehouses," and elimination of "all stocks of potatoes and vegetable seeds." A team of Harvard public health specialists issued its own report in May 1991, affirming that the destruction of the Iraqi infrastructure, particularly the elimination of 18 of its 20 electric power generating plants, created a public health catastrophe, with the civilian population suffering epidemics of gastroenteritis, typhoid, and cholera.

> Severe malnutrition is so widespread as to suggest the real possibility of famine in Iraq. . . . Hospitals and health centers have inadequate sanitation due to damage to water-purification and sewage-treatment plants. There is not enough electricity for operating rooms, diagnostic facilities, sterile procedures, and laboratory equipment.

The report adds that "Iraq's entire system of water purification and distribution relies on electricity to run water-treatment plants . . . Raw sewage continues to be pumped into the Tigris River, polluting the drinking water of densely populated areas in southern Iraq." The Harvard team notes that 55,000 deaths of Iraqi children have already been reported and projects that a staggering 170,000 Iraqi children may die by the end of the year. While some experts view this projection as inflated, a later, more comprehensive study by American and other Western experts, released on October 22, 1991, confirmed that Iraq's child mortality rate almost quadrupled after the war, leading to the likelihood of tens of thousands of additional deaths among Iraqi children under five. The study found children to be massively deprived of milk, medicine, food, and safe water — hardly surprising since Iraqi grain harvests were down 75 percent, herds of cattle and sheep were decimated by 50 percent, and two-thirds of sampled households tested positive to coloform-contaminated drinking water, the main source of typhoid and cholera. Shortly after the war, the *Boston Globe* reported "children were surviving by eating grass" and that "the disposal of corpses has been left to packs of wild dogs and swarms of flies."[32]

While initially dismissing such apocalyptic reports, the Bush administration itself acknowledged in June 1991 that Iraq faced a catastrophe and "will take years to rebuild." Administration analysts told the *New York Times* that "Iraq's electrical power industry may have been damaged well beyond the intentions of allied war planners, who developed a still-secret weapon that dropped thousands of metallic filaments onto the electrical network." Confirming that the Iraqis "were struggling precariously under a patchwork of short-term fixes that will probably deteriorate in the months ahead," Bush advisors admitted shortly after the war that tens of thousands of additional Iraqi civilians could die by 1992.[33]

The civilian catastrophe in Iraq is less surprising when it is recognized that only about 7 percent of the 88,500 tons of bombs (equivalent to five Hiroshimas) dropped on Iraq and Kuwait were "smart" laser-guided bombs boasting a hit rate, according to the military, of 90 percent. The rest, or approximately 82,000 tons of "dumb" unguided bombs, had a miss rate acknowledged to be 75 percent, suggesting 62,000 tons of bombs dropped somewhere other than on their designated targets. Journalist Holly Sklar concludes that "collateral damage—civilian death and destruction—was the norm, not the rare exception." She might have added that the destruction of power plants, electric and telephone lines, and other infrastructure was anything but accidental; such civilian lifelines, since they also service the Iraqi military, were simply reclassified by the Pentagon as military targets and frontally attacked.[34]

Remarkably, over 200,000 people died in the seven-week war, according to a comprehensive survey published in mid-1991 by the environmental activist group, Greenpeace. The survey reported that 100,000 to 120,000 Iraqi soldiers died, up to 15,000 Iraqi civilians were killed in the aerial bombardments, as many as 30,000 Kurds and other displaced people died in refugee camps and on the road, and up to 46,000 Iraqis died of disease and malnutrition in the first ten weeks following the conclusion of the war. Three hundred forty-three Allied soldiers, including 266 Americans, also died in combat or in accidents.[35]

The virtual absence of debate among the American leadership and in the media about these horrors denotes a wilding mentality. The immensely popular General Schwarzkopf, known as a humane military man, had no moral qualms about the one-sided "kill ratio"; indeed, he was proud to announce that "We easily killed more than 100,000" Iraqi soldiers, while losing only a few hundred of our own. Before the slaughter, he had told TV host David Frost: "We don't want our hands tied behind our back. We are going to do it one hundred percent all the way and do whatever is necessary to inflict maximum casualties on the enemy and minimum on our own forces . . . " General Powell expressed indifference to the number of Iraqi military dead, saying it was "really not a matter I am terribly interested in."[36]

Nor has there been official remorse about the bombing of two civilian nuclear reactors in Baghdad, the world's first attacks on operating reactors, nor about burying alive hundreds of Iraqi soldiers by dumping mountains of earth and sand into their trenches. Pentagon spokesman Pete Williams dismissed this atrocity with the comment that "War is hell." Nor have there been official regrets about the slaughter on the "highway of death" from Kuwait City to Basra, where thousands of fleeing Iraqi soldiers in the last hours of the war were carpet bombed by B-52s, FA-18 jets, and F-16 fighter-bombers. Allied pilots trapped the retreating Iraqis by disabling vehicles at the front and rear of a long convoy and then "pummeling the traffic jam for hours. Scores of Iraqis were crushed or incinerated in their vehicles." Pilots called the slaughter a "turkey shoot," "shooting fish in a barrel," "shooting ducks in a pond." Most of the pilots said they "thought the Iraqis were getting what they deserved." "I think we're past the point of just letting him get in his tanks and drive them back into Iraq and say 'I'm sorry,' " said Lt. Col. George Patrick of the U.S. Air Force, as he rested between bombing missions. Bush spokesman Marlin Fitzwater added, "You will not find America feeling guilty for Saddam Hussein's invasion and destruction of his own people." Nonetheless, some pilots were reported to have had serious moral qualms about the "turkey shoot," and American leaders were sufficiently worried about public perceptions of a horrifying massacre to mount a massive public relations compaign; as the *Washington Post* reported, this included "a hastily arranged televised statement" by President Bush in the Rose Garden indicating that Iraqi troops "were not withdrawing voluntarily and that Saddam Hussein was trying to achieve a political victory from a military rout."[37]

Zbigniew Brzezinski, national security advisor in the Carter administration, was one of the few members of the foreign policy establishment to raise questions about the morality of the Gulf war. After reviewing the UN's report of the "apocalypse," Brzezinski noted that the nightmare of the abortive Kurdish and Shiite revolts, catalyzed by the American intervention, compounded the catastrophe of the war itself. (He neglects to add postwar sanctions, aggressively promoted by President Bush, which by mid-1991 brought millions more Iraqi civilians to the brink of famine.) He suggested that "the war may have been a classical case of an underreaction to earlier signs of Mr. Hussein's aggressiveness that later prompted an overreaction to the actual act of aggression. This overreaction," he observed dryly, was morally "disproportionate." Another dissenter, Anthony Lewis of the *New York Times*, mused on the ironies of coming to the rescue of Kuwait at the expense of the abandoned Kurds, who a few years earlier had been chemically gassed by Saddam when he was still an American ally; Bush's apparent indifference when millions of Kurds, inspired by his own words, became refugees facing a potential holocaust led Lewis to comment that "Something is missing in George Bush. An empathy gene, if there were such a thing. An instinctive response to the pain of other human beings. An internal monitor that tells him when political calculation has to stop, yielding to concern for decency." This is a sad commentary on wilding sensibilities at the highest levels of government.[38]

Can such massive wilding, involving the death of 200,000, be justified? It is true that a dangerous and unacceptable act of aggression by Iraq was rebuffed and that an unprecedented community of nations opposing such aggression was mobilized. Bush's actions may have made it more difficult for future American presidents to go to war without strong support from the international community, a potentially significant contribution to a more lawful world. But even Brzezinski, well known for his tough-mindedness, raises serious questions about the ultimate legacy. America's influence in the region, and its military credibility worldwide, has been enhanced, but such self-aggrandizing ends in themselves cannot justify a devastating war that might have been avoided. Moreover, Brzezinski notes that the apparent geopolitical gains have come with heavy costs, including potential "Lebanonization" of the region, the possible perception in Arab countries that "Americans view Arab lives as worthless," and the triggering of "sensitive moral issues" about American restraint and intervention, all of which could add up to "a post-Gulf disaster."

Brzezinski does not mention other debacles such as the still unknown degree of ecological destruction caused by the biggest oil spill and the worst oil well fires in history, or the return to feudal justice in "liberated" Kuwait, where people accused of collaborating with the Iraqi occupation forces were summarily sentenced to long prison terms without legal representation and after alleged torture in jail. (As the *New York Times* reported, one man was sentenced to fifteen years for "wearing a T-shirt with President Saddam Hussein's picture on it.") In addition, the sovereign for whom the war was waged, the Emir of Kuwait, reinstalled himself in a plush estate with gold-plated bathroom faucets before he had restored running water to most of his people, while, on the political front, postponing free elections for the Kuwaiti parliament.[39]

Potentially of more serious global consequence, the presumed increase in American influence has not led to any definitive shift toward democracy or peace elsewhere in the Middle East. Shuttling across the Middle East after the war, Secretary of State Baker discovered that ancient Middle East conflicts do not yield to American notions of how the war changed the region. Despite their agreement to attend an American- and Soviet-sponsored peace conference, the most promising regional development in the months following the war, neither Israel nor its Arab antagonists, by late 1991, had softened their positions on substantive, as against procedural, issues. Israel had not abandoned its implacable opposition to a Palestinian state and the Arab nations remained hostile to Israel and deeply ambivalent about making peace. An enduring Arab-Israeli peace and settlement of the Palestinian issue would be an extraordinary accomplishment by the Bush administration, but most analysts view it as remote. As Brzezinski hints, the war may ultimately prove to have worsened ancient religious, ethnic, and racial conflicts in the region, including both the Palestinian and Kurdish problems. Moreover, only months after the war, President Bush and Congressional leaders were seriously threatening to go to war with Iraq again, to destroy Iraq's remaining capacity to produce weapons of mass destruction and finally dispose of Saddam Hussein.

In addition to the war, the other main legacy of the Bush years may be the spread of Reagan's gospel of the entrepreneur to a worldwide community of believers. The collapse of Communism has produced a new god—the free market— everywhere in the Eastern bloc. As the 1990s began, Poland, Hungary, and Czechoslovakia were being run by economists who regarded the market as the solution to everything from worker sloth to pollution. Similarly, by 1990, Mikhail Gorbachev had surrounded himself by many policymakers who were almost religious in their capitalist enthusiasms, while new leaders, such as Boris Yeltsin and Leningrad (now St. Petersburg) city council chairman Anatoly A. Sobchak, were even more zealous in their market devotions. *Shmelyov's Law*, penned by influential economist Nikolai Shmelyov, sums up the emerging Soviet mood: "Everything that is economically inefficient is immoral and everything that is economically efficient is moral"—a perfect epigram for a wilding culture. Some East European leaders sound like Ronald Reagan in their passionate public homilies to the entrepreneur and the magic of the market. Pytor S. Fillpov, an influential economist on the St. Petersburg City Council, says unabashedly, "I agree with those who say we must hurry quickly away from Marxism-Leninism, through Socialism, to Reaganism."[40]

George Bush can claim only some of the credit, but he has successfully presided over this consummate form of American imperialism. As its other exports decline, the United States' last great export may be a new seductive American Dream, whose glitter masks the culture of wilding that supports it. Rarely in history has an idea, the market, gained such global currency, at least among the world's elites. Of course, countries ranging from Japan to France to South Korea continue to rely heavily on government to compete and prosper, and it is a conceit of American leaders to imagine that their own market gospel is more than just a rhetorical tool across much of the globe. But the very magic of the rhetoric in the new, post-communist era has led conservative American thinkers to gloat about the "end of history." There can be no more serious debate about how to live, intones State Department analyst Francis Fukuyama, for around the world, peoples everywhere want to live like Americans. This should be read less as a description of reality than as one of the opening salvos in a new global war for the mind, where possibilities of thought control now exist on a planetary scale. Should the ideologues of the Bush era succeed, they will have earned the dubious honor of laying the intellectual groundwork for a global wilding culture.

5

The Dreamin' Is Easy and
the Living Is Hard
A Wilding Recipe for the 1990s

This whole world is wild at heart and weird on top.
LULA in *Wild at Heart*

THERE ARE signs, everywhere, that the culture of wilding is trickling down from Washington and Wall Street to Main Street. Civilized Boston woke up to the 1990s with headlines about the Stuart murder. A few months later headlines told of a frail fifty-seven-year-old liquor store manager, Jean Stranberg, executed by a seventeen-year-old with a sawed-off shotgun, all for a jar of Easter Seal pennies worth maybe twelve dollars. A couple of months earlier, on February 20, three Boston University students learned how wild Boston had become when as a joke they jumped on the hood of a stranger's car on campus, slightly damaging the vehicle. The driver pulled out an automatic weapon and shot Leslie J. Young, aged twenty, an engineering major, in the chest, then turned to Young's two friends and asked: "Does anybody want more?" When one said "No," the driver sped off and Young was taken in critical condition to an intensive care unit. The students had gotten a quick lesson in the importance of a man's possessions, especially expensive ones like his car.[1]

Perhaps more telling about the state of America as it entered the 1990s is not such outrageous wildings but the small wildings that ripple through our daily experiences. *Boston Globe* columnist Susan Trausch satirizes her own propensities for wilding: "An extra ten bucks dropped out of the automatic teller ma-

chine the other day and I didn't give it back." There were, after
all, Trausch explains, "no guards. No middleman . . . The
machine doesn't ask questions." She "grabbed the bills,"
Trausch writes, and stifled "the impulse to shout, 'I won!'"
Later, she thinks, "Is this why the world is a mess? People don't
want to be chumps so they say, 'I'll get mine now,' and then
they grab an illicit brownie from the pastry tray of life. And
oh, the noise we make if we don't get what we consider ours!
If, for instance, only forty dollars had come out of the slot instead of fifty dollars, my outrage would have echoed in the
aisles from aerosols to zucchini." But beating the system "made
me want to play again," Trausch admits. "Maybe there was a
gear loose. Maybe hundreds of dollars would come out."
Trausch concludes that "I'd like to report that at least the illicit
money went to charity, it didn't. I blew it on lottery tickets."[2]

Trausch's lingering moral pangs are quite unusual. One sociologist laughed after reading her story, speculating that he
and most other Americans would have pocketed the illicit
greenback without a second thought — with no flickering of the
conscience whatsoever. According to Queens, New York
school board member Jimmy Sullivan, a streetwise, savvy observer of American life in the nineties, "Everybody cheats." It
"isn't just some people," Sullivan emphasizes pointedly, "95
percent of the people. Some cheat a little. Some cheat a lot.
You work in an office, you take home supplies. People work
at a construction site, they take home two-by-fours. Unfortunately, we've become a nation of petty crooks." Admitting
to a reporter that his main concern as a school board official
was patronage jobs for his "people" — white political cronies in
his clubhouse — Sullivan makes no apologies. Everybody is doing it, cheating to get theirs, especially now that times are getting tougher. Sullivan certainly knows what he is talking
about, at least regarding the New York City school system,
where three-quarters of the city's school boards are under investigation and half are believed corrupt. Sullivan himself was
manipulating a multimillion dollar budget to build his own

corrupt school fiefdom. Sullivan explains, "We're a nation of fucks and gangsters because that's what we glorify in Americana." It's all part of the American Dream today.[3]

Sullivan may be on his way to jail, not having counted on the fact that there are still honest people like his school superintendent, Coleman Genn, who switched from working with Sullivan to wearing a hidden microphone for an independent commission investigating school corruption. Genn is part of the "second America" discussed in Chapter 1, the majority America that has been touched but not debased by the wilding epidemic and continues to struggle honorably to maintain its integrity. Sullivan, nonetheless, has his finger on a contradiction tearing American apart in the final decade of the century. The pushers of dreams, the creators of "Americana," have picked up the drumbeat from the White House, feverishly selling the Reagan-Bush high roller version of the American Dream in movies, magazines, and the ubiquitous video. While Americans are being willingly seduced, swimming in exquisitely alluring images of the pleasures only money can buy, money itself is getting harder to come by. As Americans dream big, economic shadows are lengthening and darkening. This contradiction between the glamorous life on the screen and the contracting opportunities of real life has the potential to spread the epidemic deeply into the "second America" which, until now, has kept it at bay.

Revving Up the Dream Machine

Tom Cruise, *People* magazine reports, has become the 1990s silver screen idol, the star of stars in America's most enchanting dream factory. Cruise established himself early in the 1980s, in a movie called *Risky Business*, which helped mold the fantasies of the Reagan era. Cruise played the modern suburban Huck Finn who finally makes good. A disappointment to his straight arrow parents, whose dream is to get him into Prince-

ton, Cruise seems to enjoy going on joyrides in the family
Porsche far more than studying for college boards. But one
class—on business entrepreneurship—finally does wake him
up. In a Reaganite revelation, Cruise realizes that by starting
his own sex business, he can make it big and have fun too.
When his parents pack off to a European vacation, he launches
his business in grand entrepreneurial fashion, turning the family suburban home into a whorehouse. Cruise is transformed,
the young goof-off becomes a zealously ambitious entrepreneur rivaling any Wall Street trader in his detailed attention to markets, customers, and finances. In a morality play
for his times, Cruise's business is a huge success. As young
women and clients traipse in, Cruise stands at the door count-
ing the dollars, his charming, impish grin stretching from ear
to ear. The skeptical Princeton admissions officer who comes
down to take a look is so impressed that he awards Cruise the
admission ticket to Princeton that his parents had dreamed of.

John Taylor points out the interesting contrasts between
Cruise in *Risky Business* and Dustin Hoffman in *The Graduate*,
the coming-of-age movie of the 1960s. Hoffman is tormented
by the moral ambiguities of sex and money in suburban America while Cruise just wants to cash in. The 1980s theme of
"prostitution-as-business" in *Risky Business* offers, Taylor
notes, "an astonishingly symmetric inversion of the sixties
theme of business-as-prostitution that is an undercurrent in
The Graduate."[4]

Taylor observes that Cruise is a part of a new crop of male
movie stars, such as Michael Douglas, Harrison Ford, Mel
Gibson, and Sylvester Stallone, whose roles differ strikingly
from those of the earlier generation of stars, such as Dustin
Hoffman, Al Pacino, and Robert DeNiro. In movies such as
Midnight Cowboy, *Serpico*, and *Mean Streets*, Hoffman, Pacino,
and DeNiro portrayed alienated, tormented antiheroes, struggling with and finally rejecting the values of society. In contrast, the new breed of stars are competitive "glamor boys

. . . not motivated by hostility or angst but by the desire to succeed." They do not "question themselves or society." They make a lot of money and have fun doing it, not letting moral compunctions interfere with their pleasures in winning big. In *Wall Street*, Michael Douglas's character spoke unabashedly for Ivan Boesky when he proclaimed that "greed was good."[5]

The current stars symbolize an economic revolution in Hollywood that transformed the dreams being pumped out to wide-eyed audiences. In the 1960s and early 1970s, the famous studios, Warner Bros., United Artists, MGM, and 20th Century Fox, were still independent. Politically sensitized directors often enjoyed great control, creating probing films about Vietnam, nuclear power, and other issues of the day. But by the 1980s, large multinationals had bought up virtually all the studios, installing new hard-nosed executives and business-minded producers who reined in the directors and helped rewrite the scripts. The great Hollywood Dream Machine, as Meryl Streep recently pointed out, was now securely programmed to the bottom line.[6]

At Paramount Pictures, producers Don Simpson and Jerry Bruckheimer personify the new Hollywood. Simpson and Bruckheimer collaborated on some of the most spectacular box office successes of the 1980s, including *Beverly Hills Cop, Flashdance, Top Gun*, and *Beverly Hills Cop II*. Former 1960s hippies, Simpson and Bruckheimer evolved comfortably into the spirit of the eighties. The formula they brought to all their scripts was a fantasy of competition and triumph, the individual overcoming all odds to become a big winner. In *Flashdance*, for example, made in 1983 during the height of the Reagan recession, a young, beautiful working-class dancer beats the economic odds, dancing her way out of a desolate industrial wasteland in a bleak Midwestern city to Cinderella stardom. "There are people," Simpson says, "who are successful and who win. They have moments of pain but they are winners. Then there are losers. Jerry and I side with the winners. We aren't interested

in losers. Losers are boring." Hollywood had cast its lot with
Ronald Reagan.[7]

The success of *Flashdance* was a surprise, for critics noted that
it seemed less a movie than an extended MTV rock video. But
the critics underestimated both the audience's receptivity to
Reaganite fantasy and the riveting power of the sensual video
imagery, featuring erotic close-ups of actress Jennifer Beals
pulsating to the music. The video revolution, a triumph of
high-tech engineering and high-gloss aesthetics, brings Hollywood dreams into the living room, where young children, as
well as teenagers and adults, are now programmed daily with
high-voltage visuals. We are increasingly defined, media critic
Stuart Ewen writes, by "all-consuming images," searing our
brains with almost unimaginable intensity. Never has the
American Dream, Ewen hints, been communicated with such
neurological force.[8]

Alongside Hollywood as a purveyor of the new mind-
grabbing dream stands the advertising industry, the master
producer of "all-consuming images." The line between movies
and advertising actually blurs in the Reagan-Bush era, as critic
Charles Champlin implicitly suggests in his description of a
scene from another Simpson and Bruckheimer film, *American
Gigolo*: "Nothing, neither bosom nor buttock, is photographed
more lovingly than the [Mercedes] 450SL—those taillights,
winking provocatively in the velvet night, such as to drive men
mad." Film directors increasingly function as advertisers, perhaps recognizing that they are playing to audiences addicted
to high-priced consumption. Advertisers, in turn, exploiting
the new visual technology, have become the consummate artists of the 1990s, designing the electrified commercial fantasies
that define the American way of life.[9]

Television has become the ad industry's ultimate weapon,
allowing advertisers to mainline the dream directly into the
nervous system. Sociologist Stephen Pfohl describes a young
girl "exposing herself to a television." He says, "It strikes me

that she is daydreaming with the machine. Her eyes are moving rapidly but her body remains still. She sits knees curled within her dress, biting her nails, clutching a doll. Wide eyes, it's electric." The young girl enters the room where Pfohl is talking with her mother. "Mommy, Mommy. They showed a K-TL 191 with screaming rear view blinkers and a flashing rotary rocket launcher with a digital tracking unit. It was only $29.99 but for one time only it's $19.99. But you have to call right away. Can we Mommy? Can we? . . . All you have to do is call." The little girl has memorized the toll-free number she wants her mother to dial. Pfohl concludes that as consumers we have been "seduced into taking the media within ourselves; its screens and its terminals now functioning as our most intimate organs of sensation . . . We are the media. We are the television!"[10]

In 1990, 93 percent of American girls said that shopping had become their favorite activity, far outstripping "dating, exercising, or even going to the movies." Shoppaholism, now the American addiction of choice, reflects the coming of age of conspicuous consumption, partly molded, Laurence Shames writes, by advertisers selling the high-priced Reaganite version of the American Dream. *"Top-of-the-lineness"* has become the "operative criterion," as the advertising world plies a receptive clientele with the notion that the best things in life are anything but free. Happiness, *Vogue* magazine reported in 1987, comes with "the status pen (Mont Blanc), the status loafer (Gucci) . . . the status leaf (radicchio), the status panties (Hanro), the status vinegar (balsamic), the status athletic supporter (Le Jacques), the status tennis racquet (the Prince Custom) . . . the status H_2O (Evian)." The concept is hardly new, but what today's advertisers can claim is an unprecedented ratcheting up of the fever—and the price. A top-of-the-line Piaget watch retails for three million dollars. You can buy alligator luggage for $75,000 a set, Russian sables starting at $40,000, silk sheets at $15,000 a set, or gold belts at $30,000 each.[11]

Downtime

As the price of happiness ratchets up, the ability of the average American to pay is falling. The great contradiction of the 1990s may be the increasing gap between bigger American appetites and shrinking American wallets.

The Dream Machine, while faithfully serving the Reagan-Bush vision of the good life, is on a collision course with the American economy. In 1973, for the first time ever, the real wage of the American worker began falling. "The U.S. standard of living, long the envy of the rest of the world," *Business Week* proclaimed, had "hit the wall." By the time Ronald Reagan was elected, the shape of a great economic revolution was already becoming clear. Wages were continuing to slip so rapidly that American workers could no longer support their own families. Just to stay even, both husband and wife would have to become workers, their two incomes increasingly required to do the job that one had done before.

The problem worsened in the 1980s. As Ronald Reagan began spinning his dreams of the entrepreneurial jackpot, young people woke up to the harsh possibility of downward mobility. Young men wondered whether, even with their wives working, they would be able to buy a house as big as their parents'. In many places, like Boston, Washington, and San Francisco, many doubted that they would be able to afford a house at all. "Is the American Dream about to end?" *Business Week* asked in the late 1980s. "For the first time since the depression," the magazine continued, "millions of Americans face the likelihood that they will not be able to live as well as their parents."[12]

Ronald Reagan and George Bush were elected on the promise that they would fix the economy, but the paper trail of the 1980s suggests that they may have done more than renege on their promises. America in the eighties went so deep in hock to the rest of the world (in 1988, Wall Street financier Peter J. Peterson calculated the debt at almost a half-trillion dollars) that it is losing control of its destiny. The sale of Rockefeller Center to Japanese buyers symbolized a new 1990 American reality; we are "selling off more of what this country's people own," Wellesley economist Carolyn Shaw Bell reports, simply to meet "the interest on the debt, let alone repaying any of the principal." Meanwhile, American industry in the eighties, from autos to machine tools to textiles, was being routed in international competition, so thoroughly pummeled by the Japanese, the Germans, and the Koreans that *Business Week* speculated whether "the United States is following Britain" into permanent economic decline. Harvard's Robert Reich points out that "Since the mid-1970s, America's largest five hundred industrial corporations have failed to generate a single new job." America's economy, Reich concludes, is "slowly unraveling" in a sustained decline "marked by growing unemployment, mounting business failures, and falling productivity." Economic performance under President Bush proved disastrous, with real wages falling for three straight years as of late 1991 and economic growth averaging 0.6 percent, the lowest of the postwar era. New external shocks, like a shooting up of oil prices, could accelerate America's fitful decline into a dizzy economic free-fall, precipitating sustained stagnation, recession, or even catastrophic depression in the 1990s.[13]

In the midst of this economic bad news, Americans continue to be glued to the Dream Machine, creating the paradox that *Business Week* calls the "money illusion." They keep spending as if they are "getting the kind of real raises" that they used to get "in the 1960s." Something is profoundly out of kilter, the magazine suggests, since in a period of crushing new constraints, the average American appears unable to "lower his sights."[14]

Of course, the contradiction cuts more or less deeply depending where the dreamer is perched on the economic ladder. For those on top, whether business executive or fabled yuppie, there is the problem, as the *New York Times* reported in a 1987 story, of "feeling poor on $600,000 a year." The *Times* describes the misery of young Wall Street financiers and New York doctors and lawyers feeling strapped by the costs of their million-dollar co-ops. Nonetheless the pain is tolerable, as Kevin Phillips writes, since Reaganomics unleashed an upsurge of riches to the wealthy that "has not been seen since the late nineteenth century, the era of the Vanderbilts, Morgans, and Rockefellers." As the economy declines, the rich can keep dreaming big dreams.[15]

Where the contradiction draws blood is at the bottom. The poor, no less than the rich, stay tuned in to the Dream Machine, in bad times as well as good. They are always the "last hired and the first fired," so every business cycle wreaks havoc with their dreams, and bad times in the early 1990s have been horrific. President Bush, following President Reagan's lead, systematically targeted the poor in the current downturn. The safety net was shredded, leaving many without housing, most without medical care, few with jobs or educational opportunity. Mired in Third World conditions of poverty while video-bombarded with Reaganite First World dreams, rarely has a population suffered a greater gap between socially cultivated appetites and socially available opportunities.

In the great American middle, too, blood has been drawn. *Business Week* says that Joe Sixpack found himself badly slipping as the economy faltered. He plunged into debt, thinking, "Buy now, before the price goes up again. With a little luck, he figured, his next raise would keep the credit-card bills and the mortgage covered." The problem was that "the real raises didn't get any better" as the eighties went on. Unable to "lower his sights," Joe kept "borrowing. He now owns a house, a big Japanese color TV and VCR, an American car, and a Korean personal computer — all bought on credit." His wife is working, which help pays the "children's orthodontist bills and family entertainment, but it falls short of what they'll need to send the kids to college." Judith Batemen, the wife of a Michigan Bell Telephone dispatcher, told *Business Week* that the couple runs a big weekly "deficit," but until times get better, which she keeps hoping will happen, she says, "We enter a lot of sweep-stakes." Larry Williams, laid off from a well-paid factory super-visory position and now a security guard at Brigham and Women's Hospital in Boston, is less optimistic and sounds less benign: "Sometimes I get real touchy when I'm not working. I've been working since I was eighteen years old. The first week was like a vacation, but when you get into a month, you start getting real edgy, you know what I mean?"[16]

"I'm Gonna Get Mine": America Goes Wild

It is not a long stretch from Larry Williams' "edgy" feeling, to anger and cynicism, to wilding. Feeling that his old job is per-manently gone, since manufacturing in this country is in his view "down the tubes," Williams is finding it harder to match his life to his dreams. His feelings are shared by millions of Americans whose dreams are threatened. Evidence is mount-ing that many are recruits to the culture of wilding, people in an era of decline who are prepared to do whatever it increasing-ly takes to make it.

Drawing on a national survey, Boston University professors Donald Kanter and Philip Mirvis report that the wilding mind-set has spread across America. The American dream of indivi-dual initiative is degrading into the cynical maxim of "I will do anything to get ahead and not be left behind." Self-interest, Kanter and Mirvis believe, has become such an overweening urge that it is pushing empathy and moral sensibilities into the far background. They describe an American landscape in which close to half of the population takes as their basic as-sumption "that most people are only out for themselves and that you are better off zapping them before they do it to you."[17]

Many Americans, Kanter and Mirvis report, believe that their fellow Americans will cheat, lie, and dissimulate to get what they want, especially where money is concerned. Sixty percent say that they expect "people will tell a lie if they can gain by it," and 62 percent say that "people claim to have ethical standards, but few stick to them when money is at stake." About half say that "an unselfish person is taken advantage of in today's world," and slightly under half believe that people "inwardly dislike putting themselves out to help other people." As among the Ik, who take positive pleasure in hurting others, none of this strikes Americans as particularly noteworthy or suprising. Forty-three percent — and more than half of young people under twenty-four — see selfishness and fakery at the core of human nature. Millions of Americans, Kanter and Mirvis conclude, are hard-boiled cynics who, "to put it simply, believe that lying, putting on a false face, and doing whatever it takes to make a buck" are all part of the nature of things.[18]

Kanter and Mirvis dissected wilding types at every economic level. At the top are a depressing variety of groups eager to exploit the new opportunities the Reagan-Bush era has opened up for them, including "command cynics," senior managers who are "jungle fighters" and "subscribe to the Darwinian logic that they 'made it,' so everyone else must be weak, naive, inept, or just plain dumb." They believe that "everyone has a price and can be bought." The "administrative sideliners" are another school: mid- to upper-level bureaucrats, whose "view of human nature is predominantly cold" and who "have no real concern for people, save as instruments" for their own ends. Then there are "articulate players," mostly young professionals, who became the most visible symbols of greed in the eighties. They live in the self-oriented world that Christopher Lasch described as the "culture of narcissism." What they have in common "is a willingness to do whatever has to be done to others in order to advance." They are metaphorically "porcupines whose quills are at the ready," taking pleasure in their capacity to put others down on their road to the top.[19]

Toward the middle and lower ends of the hierarchy are other groups, many impaled on the sharp edge of economic change and decline. Among them are the "squeezed cynics," often sons and daughters of skilled workers or lower-middle-class clericals, whose once bright aspirations "have faded along with the decline of heavy industry. The jobs they expected have been automated, eliminated, or sent overseas." Downwardly mobile, they exhibit a "dead-ender's self-interest," whose anthem is "Where's mine?" and "What's in it for me?" Then there are the "obstinate stoics," disproportionately blue-collar, who "do not trust people . . . and seem to feel more strongly than most that expecting anyone to help you makes you a damn fool." And finally there are the "hard-bitten cynics," mainly shopfloor workers and unskilled laborers, who live "on the razor's edge between independent respectability and antisocial aggression." Among their life-guiding maxims: "Never give money to anyone who needs it."[20]

Kanter and Mirvis seem unsurprised by their findings. The intensely self-centered, antisocial mind-set they uncovered reflects the successes of socialization rather than its failure. Making reference to the culture of the Reagan-Bush era, Kanter argues, "The tendency to behave cynically is being reinforced to an unprecedented degree by a social environment that seems to have abandoned idealism and increasingly celebrates the virtue of being 'realistic' in an impersonal, acquisitive tough-guy world." He might have been talking about the Ik when he concludes that "In citizen and country alike, there seems to be a loss of faith in people and in the very concept of community."[21]

Young and Wild

The young are among the more exuberant wilders in America. Progeny of the Reagan-Bush era, and the most vulnerable to the slings of economic fortune, they are an ominous harbinger of America's future.

Kanter and Mirvis report that a clear majority of youth under twenty-four, in contrast to only 43 percent of the population as a whole, are "unvarnished cynics" who view "selfishness as fundamental to people's character." Most students do not disagree with this assessment of their generation. On the first day of the 1990 spring semester, I asked a class of about forty, mainly economics majors, whether the "average" student on campus would agree or disagree with a series of highly charged statements about selfishness and self-interest. Their answers were not reassuring. Two-thirds said that the average student would agree that "There is nothing more important to me than my own economic well-being," while 72 percent said that the typical student would agree that "I am not responsible for my neighbor." Three-fourths said their generation believed that "It's everyone for himself or herself in the American economy," and 88 percent said their fellow students would agree with the notion that "In our society everyone has to look out for number one." A stunning 96 percent thought their generation believed that "Competition is the most important virtue in a market society," and two-thirds expected a typical student to agree that "People do not let moral scruples get in the way of their own advancement." In discussion, they explained that most students were apprehensive about their economic prospects, fearing that they would not do as well as their parents. If they wanted to succeed, they said, they would have to focus all their energies on "buttering their own bread."[22]

On the positive side, significantly lower percentages of the students, ranging from one-third to one-half, said that they personally subscribed to the selfish sentiments just enumerated. This is an indication that a significant sector of the younger generation may remain committed to moral principles. My own impression as a teacher is that a large percentage of today's college students remain generous and decent, although increasingly confused and torn between "making it" and remaining faithful to their moral ideals.

Growing student cynicism is leading to an explosion of wilding on campuses across the country. A report by the Carnegie Foundation for the Advancement of Teaching, released in 1990, found "a breakdown of civility and other disruptive forces" that is leaving campus life "in tatters." Of special concern is an epidemic of cheating, as well as a mushrooming number of racial attacks, rapes, and other "hate crimes." Words, the currency of the university, are increasingly "used not as the key to understanding, but as weapons of assault."[23]

Ernest L. Boyer, Carnegie's president, said that college promotional material "masks disturbing realities of student life," mirroring the "hard-edged competitive world" of the larger society.[24] Desperate for good grades, huge numbers of students routinely plagiarize papers and cheat on exams. Studies on many campuses, including Indiana University and the University of Tennessee, show that a majority of students admit to submitting papers others wrote or copying large sections of friends' papers. A majority also confesses to looking at other students' answers during in-class exams. In the spring of 1991, seventy-three students in an introductory computer programming course were disciplined for participating in the largest cheating scandal in the history of the prestigious Massachussetts Institute of Technology. "You could check for cheating in any class and you'd certainly find a significant portion of the people cheating," one MIT student said, adding casually that "It's one way of getting through MIT." [25]

While a significant minority of students are idealistic and intensely concerned with others, the majority appear increasingly cynical about their studies and their futures. They want to "invest as little time in their studies as possible," the Carnegie report suggests, while collecting their meal ticket and moving on to the professional gravy train. Fifty-five percent of faculty members complained that "Most undergraduates in my institution only do enough to get by." Carnegie president Boyer, however, noted that faculty are complicit in the problem by pursuing "their own research at the expense of teaching." He might have added that some faculty and administrators are providing the worst role models, as evidenced by the growing scandal in faculty research. Congressman John Dingell has uncovered science fraud in the biology labs of MIT as well as unlawful diversion of research overhead expenditures for such things as "flowers, country-club memberships, and going away parties for departing deans" in many of the nation's most famous universities, including Harvard, Stanford, and the California Institute of Technology. Stanford University president Donald Kennedy resigned in 1991 after the media reported the extensive diversion of Stanford overhead funds to pay for such extravagances as a yacht. The reputation of Nobel Laureate David Baltimore, one of the country's foremost cancer researchers and president of Rockefeller University, has been tarnished by the National Institute of Health's conclusion that there was falsification of data by a member of Baltimore's own laboratory. Campus life breaks down as each campus estate follows the narrow path of its own career dictates.[26]

Today's student culture transparently reflects the intensely materialistic, entrepreneurial ethos of the Reagan-Bush era. Elite institutions, where the Carnegie report finds the most "acute" problems, are filled with students driving expensive cars and wearing designer clothes. The Dream Machine starts its work on them early. "It was probably inevitable," the *Boston Globe* reports, "that the baroque and pricey strollers of the eighties would be followed by a children's magazine boom in the nineties." Samir Hasni, a University of Mississippi journalism professor estimates that "twenty-five magazines for kids have been created since 1985," most aimed "at the children of yuppies." Hasni describes their parents as the "guilty generation," who are "loading their children down with money," partly as compensation for ignoring them while pushing ahead in their careers. One magazine, formerly called *Penny Power*, now renamed *Zillions*, helps kids think about what to buy, offering reviews of such goodies as Reebok's Pump, a new $170 sneaker. Many of the magazines "are spin-offs of movies, TV, and toys," marketing accessories for Barbie dolls, for example. Others help kids think smart about their investments in pricey baseball autographs and baseball cards.[27]

Growing up has lost its innocence. Unlike previous genera-

tions, today's students experience the "great American pas-
time" as an arena in which to cut their entrepreneurial baby
teeth. In a baseball store in Arlington, Massachusetts, nine-
year-old David Haroz and his buddies Rich Phillips, aged ten,
and Marc Chalufour, aged thirteen, are rifling through piles
of baseball cards to find speculative bargains. Marc is betting
on a "rookie sleeper—Jose Gonzales of Texas, worth three to
eight cents today—that Marc's dad thinks will move up smartly
in value." David's mother, Betsy Edmunds, tells a reporter that
"It's like the stock market to them. Very speculative. They
know the values." It's possible to make some big killings with
cards that hit the jackpot. A collector in Chicago recently paid
$115,000 for a vintage Honus Wagner. Most kids, of course,
play for smaller stakes, happy to deal in the glitzy holographic
card market where they can buy an Upper Deck set for forty-
eight dollars. Some, like Mark Perry of Chelsea, aged twenty-
five, invest for the long haul. Perry started at age seven and
stores a treasure lode of over 12,000 cards in his closets. When
this generation of youth talks about knowing the score, they
are not talking about which team got more runs.[28]

The *New York Times*, in the summer of 1990, reported that
the materialistic preoccupations of the young are turning them
into the generation "that couldn't care less." The *Times* article
refers to a conversation in which a young Ohio cashier, hearing
a radio news report about the missing dead and wounded in
a flash flood, looked up and said, "I wish they'd stop talking
about it. I'm sick of hearing about it." Indifference to other's
pain, pollsters suggest, typifies an alarming number of the
young. They don't want to hear about it unless "it's knocking
on my door." Young people themselves admit their self-preoc-
cupation and indifference, talking "incessantly of stress—their
preoccupation with getting jobs or grades and their concern
about personal threats like AIDS or drugs."[29]

Pollster Andrew Kohut, summarizing his own 1990 national
survey, unkindly describes the young as a "generation of self-
centered know-nothings." Only about one-fourth put a priority

on "helping make the community a better place," and many are "so self-absorbed" that they would not act to help others even in the most dire emergency. Youth, Kohut concludes pessimistically, are harbingers of a new "Age of Indifference."

All-American Drug Dealing: Wilding at the Bottom

"I spend long hours, night and day, in crack houses and on drug-copping corners, observing, befriending, and interviewing street dealers, addicts, and anyone else who will pause to talk to me." Those are the words of anthropologist Philippe Bourgois, who spent five years living in an East Harlem tenement, but he was not looking to score a big drug deal, he was trying to get inside the mind of the crack dealer and see what makes him tick. His conclusions are remarkable, suggesting that the inner-city kids on the streets bear a greater resemblance to careerist kids in college than anyone had imagined. Wilding at the bottom springs from the same basic recipe as wilding higher up.[30]

Bourgois describes a broken social world reminiscent of the Ik. Violence is everywhere, especially among people working or living with each other. Jackie was eight months pregnant when her crack-dealing husband, a drug lord of substantial means, was caught and sentenced to jail. Before he left, she shot him in the stomach, in front of his helpers. Instead of leaving her money before he was sent "upstate," he had been squandering thousands on young women and "bragging about it."[31]

Jackie's violence sufficiently impressed the new drug lord that he hired her. About the same time, Jackie started going with Julio, another dealer, who was being stalked by the lover of his ex-girlfriend, Rose, for refusing to pay her after he got her pregnant. Julio knew how to deal with violence, for he had been hired to guard a crack den where murderous stick-ups are common. On one occasion, Julio admitted "that he had been very nervous when robbers held a gun to his temple and asked for money and crack." Julio made an impression on his boss when he showed that he had successfully hidden some of the stash in a hollowed-out statue of a saint. But he did not tell his boss the true story. Julio "exaggerated to his boss the amount that had been stolen; he pocketed the difference himself."[32]

Julio had started out straight, working as a messenger for a magazine. There were no career possibilities for him there, and when he needed money to support a new crack habit, he realized he needed a better job fast. Like other crack dealers Bourgois got to know, Julio had become fed up with the "low wages and bad treatment" of the jobs available to him. He had bigger dreams of a career "offering superior wages and a dignified workplace," and he found it in the underground economy. After he started dealing crack, the money and new sense of "responsibility, success, and prestige" allowed him to kick his own crack habit.[33]

Bourgois concluded from his talks with Julio and other dealers that the view that

> the poor have been badly socialized and do not share mainstream values is wrong. On the contrary, ambitious, energetic inner-city youth are attracted to the underground [drug dealing] economy precisely because they believe in the rags-to-riches American Dream. Like many in the mainstream, they are frantically trying to get their piece of the pie as fast as possible.[34]

Drug dealers such as Julio, Bourgois finds, are meticulously following the "model for upward mobility" in the Reagan-Bush era: "aggressively setting themselves up as private entrepreneurs." Their dreams of wealth and success are precisely those of other youngsters tuned into the glitter of television and video. Rather than abandoning the dream when the hard reality of their economic world sets in, they adapt an ambitious strategy consistent with the opportunities open to them.

Bourgois hints that it is hard to distinguish these street entrepreneurs from those in business schools or already on Wall Street. They are equally dedicated to "making it" and equally ruthless in their business dealings. They are prepared to take unusual risks to realize their dream of fast money. The successful ones enjoy the same life-style, speeding "around in well-waxed Lincoln Continentals or Mercedes-Benzes." They invite friends and acquaintances "out to dinner in expensive restaurants almost every night." When a dealer parks his car on the street, "a bevy of attentive men and women . . . run to open the door for him."[35]

"Using the channels available," people such as Julio can be seen, Bourgois writes, "as rugged individualists on an unpredictable frontier where fortune, fame, and destruction are all just around the corner."[36] Widely presumed to be the archenemy of the American way of life, inner-city drug wilders are among the purest products of the American Dream.

6
Killing Society
The Ungluing of America

A nation never falls but by suicide.
RALPH WALDO EMERSON

THE WILDING EPIDEMIC has brought American society to a
critical divide. American cities and families, for several
decades in a state of decline, are now beginning to unravel
rapidly. If the forces behind American wilding are allowed to
grow, it is not impossible that the fabric of American social life
will decompose.

As I have argued, a degraded individualism lies at the root
of this decline. Since 1980, excessive economic individualism
has been the leading factor, taking the form of what I call the
Adam Smith fallacy. Adam Smith, the first great economist of
the modern age, articulated the idea of the "invisible hand,"
the market mechanism that automatically translated the selfish
ambition of each person into the good of all. Always a
problematic doctrine, in the Reagan-Bush era it has been spun
into a dream with almost surreal dimensions. In the good society, a market society, Americans now learn, the supreme virtue
is to concentrate feverishly on one's own interests, for by doing
so one not only maximizes one's chances of getting ahead, but
also performs what George Gilder, as discussed in Chapter 3,
calls a great "gift" to society. As with the Ik, goodness, in practice, means "filling one's own stomach"; the difference is that
an Ik does not pretend that such "goodness" is good for anyone
but himself or herself.

An American Dream that does not spell out the moral consequences of unmitigated self-interest threatens to turn the next

generation of Americans into wilding machines. In a pattern already visible today, Americans could turn not only on each other but on society, too self-absorbed to make the commitments and observe the moral constraints that glue together stable communities. There is abundant evidence already that a wilder generation of Americans is assaulting and abandoning society, allowing the guarantees of civilized behavior and the most vital social institutions to languish and die as they pursue their unrequited dreams.

The breakdown of society that I describe in this chapter— violence on the streets, family dissolution, chaos in government—is cause as well as consequence of the wilding crisis. As discussed in the first chapter, the wilding culture poisons families, workplaces, and other institutions, which in their weakened form spawn more wilding. There is no first cause in this chicken and egg causal chain; the wilding virus creates social breakdown and simultaneously grows out of it.

Civilization at the Breakpoint: Wilding in the Streets and the Unraveling of Society

America's culture of wilding, at its extreme, is triggering an epidemic of bizarre and terrifying violence. The new violence constitutes a direct assault on society, undermining the "social infrastructure" that sustains civilized life.

In November 1989, the *New York Times* reported that ten teenage girls were arrested and "charged with jabbing women with pins in dozens of unprovoked attacks on the Upper West Side over a one-week period." The girls "thought it was fun to run down Broadway," Deputy Police Chief Ronald Fenrich said, and stick "women with pins to see their reactions." The girls expressed some remorse, Fenrich said, although mainly "they were sorry they got caught." Meanwhile, the neighborhood residents, while they had seen more vicious crimes, told reporters that they found the pinprick attacks an "intolerable invasion, both because of the cavalier manner in which the attacks were carried out, and because rumors spread early that it was possible the jabs had come from AIDS-infected needles."[1]

American cities have always been violent places, but the pinprick attacks symbolize a new, more menacing violence and a more profound breakdown of social life. Like the "expressive wilding" in Central Park, it suggests mainly pleasure in the inflicting of pain and complete indifference to the sensibilities of the victims. For the potential targets, anyone walking the street, the message is to remain hyper-vigilant and assume that each fellow pedestrian is a threat.

A new phenomenon of "bystander" killings carries a similar message that no place is safe and that society has become too weak to offer protection. In 1987, Darlene Tiffany Moore, a visitor to Boston, was killed by a stray bullet from gang shooting while sitting on a front porch. By 1990, so many Bostonians had been hit by randomly ricocheting bullets, often inside their own homes, that forty-seven-year-old Dorothy Ingram "sleeps on the floor, fearing stray bullets may come through her windows at night."[2]

The sheer volume of violence is also new. A resident of Ingram's neighborhood says that "The past whole year of 1990 has been killing, killing, killing; somebody got shot, somebody got stabbed. That's all I've been hearing since 1990 began." There is a new expression in Boston neighborhoods, "twenty-four-and-seven-kids," referring to "children whose mothers keep them in the house twenty-four hours a day, seven days a week, because they fear for their safety." Children themselves are terrified in many neighborhoods. Fourteen-year-old Chirll Rivers is a Boston student who says she's scared: "I don't want to die. You have to watch your back every day. Someone could mistake you for someone else and shoot you. I could be the wrong person."[3] Another kid, forced to walk home from a youth program after a van broke down, collapsed in a panic, "I can't walk home, I just can't walk home. Someone got killed on my street. I'll get killed too." The *Boston Globe* reported that this youth got home, "running all the way," but in the next eight days, three young men did not have the same luck, killed on the same street, while a fourth "was fatally shot through the window of his mother's apartment." The result of this un-precedented epidemic of violence, the *Globe* said, was that "in-creasing numbers of city youths are arming themselves, carrying small knives and pistols tucked into their waistbands or inside their coats."[4]

Omaha police chief James Skinner consoled Bostonians that they have plenty of company. "Yes, you're suffering. Yes, it hurts," Skinner said, "but Boston is not alone, it's not unique." The 1990 data bear Skinner out, for Washington D.C., Atlan-ta, Baltimore, Dallas, Miami, Philadelphia, St. Louis, and fourteen other cities all had greater homicide rates than Bos-ton; indeed, Boston's 143 murders, one for every 4000 resi-dents, was only one-third the rate of Washington D.C. and one-half the rate of Dallas. In New York City, Mayor Dinkens had to order increased police funding in 1990 after the *New York Times* reported at mid-year that nineteen cabbies had already been murdered, that four children had been killed within the week in their apartments by stray bullets (called by the tabloids the "Slaughter of the Innocents"), and a sleeping baby had been wounded when a bullet went through the wall of his apartment. Describing it as an unacceptable "surge of violence," Dinkens had to take money away from schools, city hospitals, and pub-lic transportation to finance additions to the 26,000 police al-ready in the force. Felix Rohatyn, the financier known as the man who helped save New York in the 1970s, feels that far more needs to be done, saying "There is no part of the city where the quality of life is acceptable." Perhaps influenced by the fact that his wife was robbed three times in the last few years, once by a bicyclist who ripped a gold chain off her neck on Madison Avenue and another time by a thief who stole her wallet from her handbag on Fifth Avenue, Rohatyn said "There is a qualitative difference today . . . what you feel is the constant threat of something that's going to happen to you. It's not civilized life to consider yourself lucky when you've been mugged but haven't been killed." Rohatyn says it would not be hard for him to relocate his business to Denver, but there he would not find things much better. Many Denverites, like Philip Connaghan, a machine shop owner, feel they are in a "war for survival." After his shop was burglarized eight times in the last two years, Connaghan rigged up a shotgun booby trap (a single barrel shotgun propped up and attached to a tripwire), which led to the death of Michael McComb, when he tried to break in. Connaghan was fined $2,500 and ordered to pay $7,000 restitution to McComb's family, but he received overwhelming support from Denver residents fed up with crime.[5]

It is not only city life, however, that is being subverted by the new wilding. Paul Crawford, a national park ranger who now wears a .357 magnum revolver on his hip, as well as a billy club and handcuffs, says, "Fighting, stealing, killing, we get it all. People drop their guard when they come to the parks, and that's why the criminals follow them here." John C. Benjamin, a district ranger agrees. "I thought I'd be out here protecting the environment." Benjamin says. "I had no idea I would be breaking up bar fights, investigating murders and making reports on assaults."[6]

National park officials in Washington have called for bulletproof vests for their rangers. "Things have gotten a lot more intense," says Robert C. Mariott. "It used to be that we'd run into a belligerent drunk occasionally. But now," says Mariott, rangers routinely "run into people who are confrontational and violent." Ranger Robert L. McGhee was shot to death in Mississippi after "making a traffic stop on a park road." Drug rings have been uncovered in several national parks, and officials say that the parks have become stalking grounds for bands of thieves hunting autos, camera equipment, and jewelry.[7]

People come to national parks to restore their faith in society. A Detroit truck driver says one of the reasons he likes camping is that in the park you "can leave things in the tent . . . It's not like the city, where you have to lock everything up." But Jenn DeRosa, a New Jerseyite who camped across the country with her friend Steve Grillo and had her bicycle, money, and all her credit cards stolen, today prepares for camping as if she were a hardened inner-city dweller. "I feel pretty safe," DeRosa says, because now she carries "a knife" and "a stick."[8]

All over the country, people are plagued by an intensifying fear of violence. The Figgie Report, a national survey on fear of crime, indicates that four of five Americans "are afraid of being assaulted, robbed, raped, or murdered." An estimated ninety percent of Americans lock their doors, and more than half "dress plainly" to avoid attracting the attention of violent criminals. Over fifty million households stock guns, including a rapidly growing arsenal of automatic assault weapons, to ward off attack[9]

Violence has always been endemic in the United States but national statistics suggest we are entering a new era. The rate of violent crime soared 10.3 percent between 1989 and 1990, hitting a record rate of 732 violent crimes per 100,000 Americans. The data are most dramatic among youth. Psychologist Charles Patrick Ewing reports a burgeoning epidemic of murders by juveniles. "I'm terribly pessimistic," Ewing said. He showed that the number of murders by youths doubled between 1984 and 1990 and "will likely quadruple by the end of the century." Youth suicide is also at a near all-time high. In 1990 it was more than double the rate of 1970. Paul Bracy, director of the Massachusetts Department of Health's Office of Violence says flatly that "The youth violence we're experiencing in this country has never been to this level before." The *Journal of the American Medical Association* reports that the toll is enormous, with almost four of every five deaths among youth between fifteen and twenty-four years old due to accidents, homicides and suicides.[10]

The young, however, are only following their elders, who made 1990, in the words of Delaware senator Joseph Biden, "the bloodiest year in American history," with 23,438 murders, a murder rate of about 10.5 per 100,000 people. This not only is the highest rate in American history, almost 2.5 times the number of murders in 1960, but it makes America, in the words of a Senate judiciary report, "by far the most murderous industrialized nation in the world." British, Japanese, and West Germans murder each other about one-tenth as often as Americans do.[11]

The Unglued Family: Heartless Haven in a Heartless World

One of the remarkable things about Ik society was the complete unraveling of the family. Consumed by the desperate quest to get food, an Ik views family obligations as "insane." Family members, the Ik believe, are either "burdens" or competitors, in either case an obstacle to filling one's own stomach. The Ik are quick to cast off old parents and children, whom they view as "useless appendages." Bila, an unexceptional Ik mother, frequently took her baby to the fields, hoping a predator would take it away. When a leopard finally made off with it, she "was delighted. She was rid of the child and no longer had to carry it about and feed it."[12]

An extreme wilding culture spells death for the family, as it does for society as a whole. The family is ultimately a set of demanding social obligations and commitments, requiring a sense of moral obligation and a robust capacity to think beyond oneself.

America's own wilding culture seems at first blush to be reinforcing the family rather than subverting it. Wilding has made the outside world a dangerous place. To protect themselves, journalist Chris Black writes, "Citizens have hunkered down with their nuclear families and turned their homes into suburban bunkers against the threats" outside. Sociologist Ray Oldenburg says that as the sense of community erodes and the city streets become scary, "We have replaced the ideal community with the ideal private home." Americans try to keep off the streets, spending time with family rather than friends, watching videos at home rather than venturing out to the movies. Marketing consultant Faith Popcorn calls the trend "cocooning," escaping into the warm bosom of one's own family and home in order to tune out the rest of the world. The family, in Christopher Lasch's phrase, beckons as the only "haven in a heartless world."[13]

Families, however, are always more a mirror of the outside world than a barrier against it, and wilding on the outside is helping to unglue the American family, turning it into an unstable and increasingly heartless haven. As Americans harden themselves to survive on the streets and compete at work, they make more conditional family commitments and may be becoming more indifferent and assaultive toward the people they are closest to. Taking violence as one indicator, veteran researchers Richard J. Gelles and Murray A. Straus, who conducted national surveys of family violence in 1975 and 1985, report, "The cruel irony of staying home because one fears violence in the streets is that the real danger of personal attack is *in the home*. Offenders are not strangers climbing through windows, but loved ones, family members."[14]

In 1990, approximately 5000 Americans murdered someone in their immediate family—about half of these dispatching a spouse and the other half a parent, child, or sibling—accounting for almost one-fourth of all murders in the country. A staggering number of Americans are physically assaulted by family members each year, including over 1.5 million elderly victims and over 2 million children, as well as more than 2 million wives who are severely beaten by their husbands. In America a wife is beaten, the FBI estimates, every thirty seconds, and over 40 percent of the most brutally beaten, according to researchers William Stacey and Anson Shupe, are pregnant at the time. As for children, the greatest threat comes not from strangers, the *Boston Globe* reports, "but overwhelmingly from their families," where new forms of abuse are on the rise. Despite all the publicity on TV and milk cartons about strangers snatching kids, the *Globe* notes, there are no more than 300 such cases a year, while there are now "more than 160,000 family abductions annually, and nearly 60,000 youngsters expelled from their homes and refused reentry." Typical of elderly victims, who get less public attention than battered spouses or abused or abandoned children, is a seventy-seven-year-old California woman who told police her son repeatedly "hit her on the head with beer bottles," a seventy-one-year-old Massachusetts man who "suffered a six-inch gash in his forehead when his son struck him with a frying pan," and an eighty-year-old California grandmother who was imprisoned by her grandsons. She was "isolated from all outside contact" while they cashed her Social Security checks and depleted her bank account.[15]

Representative Edward R. Roybal of California, reporting a House Aging Committee finding of a 50 percent increase in family violence against the elderly from 1980 to 1990, calls it a "crisis of epic proportions." Similarly, official statistics show astronomical increases, anywhere from double to quadruple since the mid-1970s, in the rate of child abuse. It is impossible to be certain that family violence is increasing, for the figures may simply reflect better reporting techniques. Nor do we know that the modern American family is more violent than families through history, which have always been "cradles of violence." In ancient civilizations, including the Greek and Roman, as well as among the Gauls, Celts, and Scandinavians, newborn babies were routinely drowned in rivers, abandoned as prey for birds or other predators, and buried in dung piles. One historian concludes that a large percentage of eighteenth-century European and American children, subjected to routine beatings and indentured labor, would be considered "battered children" today.[16]

Whether or not it is becoming more violent, the American family is clearly becoming a less stable institution, the traditional bonds between spouses and between parents and children eroding so rapidly that some fear the nuclear family may not survive the next century. Senator Patrick Moynihan, reviewing evidence that only 6 percent of black children and 30 percent of white children will grow up with both parents, says we are already in a "postmarital" society. "The scale of marital breakdown," writes historian Laurence Stone, "has no historical precedent that I know of, and seems unique. There has been nothing like it for the last 2,000 years, and probably much longer."[17]

At least three long-term, unambiguous trends signal a dramatic ungluing of the family as we have known it: sustained high rates of divorce, a precipitous increase in the number of single-parent households, and an extraordinary increase in the numbers living outside of any family structure. Demographer James R. Wetzel reports that divorce rates are now holding steady at double those "of the average for the 1950–1964 period, and about triple the average of the 1920s and 1930s." Wetzel estimates that "more than half of all marriages contracted during the 1970s will end in divorce." Among young people marrying today between ages eighteen and twenty-four, approximately three-fourths will divorce. Marriage is no longer "for better or for worse," but on average for about seven years, after which time a declining number of divorcees will marry again, with an even higher probability of divorcing again. This decisive breakdown in permanent relationships may be, as Stone suggests, the most important revolution of modern times, a "watershed in the culture of the West."[18]

The number of single-parent households is another revolutionary development, with nearly 14 million such truncated families in 1989. This is almost triple the number in 1950 and, remarkably, is nearly half of the number of "normal" families, that is, the approximately 32 million traditional households with two parents and children. The number of mothers raising kids without a husband present has exploded from about 3.5 million in 1950 to appoximately 12 million in 1989, including a rapidly growing number of white as well as black women. Demographer Thomas Exter projects a continued mushrooming of such "incomplete" families, with numbers estimated to soar another 16 percent by the year 2000.[19]

Perhaps the most dramatic signal of family unraveling is the numbers living outside any family system. "Families were the order of the day early in the twentieth century," Wetzel writes, and as late as 1940, only about 7.5 percent of Americans lived outside of a family. Today, almost 30 percent of households are made up of single or unrelated people and almost 22 million Americans now live alone.[20]

The ungluing of the family has been visible for decades but in the last two decades has been accelerating at an extraordinary pace. The number of single mothers, for example, rose 53 percent from 1950 to 1970, and then increased an astonishing 98 percent between 1970 and 1989. The number of never-married mothers exploded tenfold during the same period, and the percentage of babies born out of wedlock mushroomed from about 5 percent of all births in 1960 to a stunning 26 percent in 1988, constituting over a million new-borns, one out of every four births, in that year alone.[21]

The same trends are taking place in European countries and Japan as well, but the rate in America is out of whack. The divorce rate in the United States is higher than that of any other country in the world, four times as high as in Japan, triple that in England and France, and double that in Denmark or Sweden. The percentage of American single-parent households is also the highest, almost quadruple that of Japan, almost three times that of Sweden, and double that of England. Moreover, the American rate of increase in single parents far outstrips that of any other country.[22]

Family ungluing, particularly divorce, reflects the most radical individualistic currents of the modern era, currents far more powerful in America than anywhere else. Traditional family obligations are becoming too confining for a growing segment of Americans. Stone argues that since 1960 American "spouses are being traded in almost as cheaply and easily as used cars," reflecting "a moral and cultural shift to untram-

meled individualism." This is consistent with a long-term cultural revolution in which people withdraw some of their attach-
ments to their communities in order to leverage more freedom
for themselves. As early as 1853, Horace Greeley warned of ris-
ing divorce as a by-product of an American individualism
evolving into virulent egotism, "wherein the Sovereignty of the
Individual—that is the right of every man to do pretty nearly
as he pleases . . . is visibly gaining ground daily."[23]

As individualism intensifies, the balance of commitment
can tilt so far toward the self that the family and other building
blocks of society decompose. When individualism turns into
rampant wilding, as among the Ik, the family is shredded, leaving atomized individuals to prey upon each other. In the
Reagan-Bush era, as the line between individualism and wilding blurs, the American family suffers its own form of abandonment, strained to the breaking point not only by acute
economic pressures but by the burden of its members' self-
preoccupation. Americans converted to the reigning ideology
of "looking after number one" are proving ready to sacrifice not
only outsiders but their kin on the altar of their own needs and
pleasures. Divorce court judge Edward M. Ginsburg concludes that the people passing through his courtroom are so
committed to putting their own happiness first that it sometimes reminds him of Rome "just before it all came undone."
Ginsburg muses that the role of the family has changed from
caring for children to being "eternally in love and having a good
time."[24]

Abandonment is the thread common to divorce and broken
households. Both reflect choices to preserve the self and enhance personal happiness at the expense of the family unit, a
choice that may be rational where no children are involved,
but frequently proves catastrophic when they are. L. J. Weitzman, in her study of the children of the divorced, finds that
they tend to feel abandoned, often traumatically so. They, indeed, *are* an abandoned population, if only because divorce is
typically "financially a severe blow" for children, who lose the

full economic as well as emotional support of two parents. Disruptions such as sale of the family home "adds to the trauma of children," Laurence Stone notes, "who may find themselves suddenly deprived not only of their father but also of their home, their school, their friends, and their economic comforts." Summarizing research findings, *Newsweek* concludes that "divorce has left a devastated generation in its wake."[25]

The experience of stepfamilies shows that the family, once dismantled, is not easily put together again. Testimony to the new age of serial marriage, one-third of all children born in the 1980s live with a stepparent and more than 7 million kids now live in stepfamilies, often composed of conglomerates of children from several past marriages. Sociologist Frank Furstenberg says that "one of the consistent findings in research is that stepparenthood does not recreate the nuclear family. It does not put the family back together again, in Humpty-Dumpty fashion." Researcher Nicholas Zill says that, psychologically, kids in stepfamilies "most resemble kids in single-parent families — even though they may be living in two-parent households." The kids often "feel they've been cast in an outsider role," says Zill, who adds that as a group stepchildren have more emotional and developmental problems and "are more likely to be victims of child abuse, especially sexual abuse." Furstenberg notes that in the stepfamily it is problematic "whether the people we count as kin can be counted on." For one thing, second marriages break up even more than first marriages, at an extraordinary 60 to 70 percent divorce rate. "Remarriages are very fragile," says Johns Hopkins researcher Andrew Cherlin. "These couples have gone through one bad marriage and they're determined not to go through another. Their antennae are up . . . and they're prepared to leave." Moreover, many stepparents can truly not be counted on as parents. Esther, a high school senior in Chicago, says of her stepmother, "It's like having a permanent guest."[26]

The abandonment of children is clearest in single-parent households, whose meteoric upsurge reflects the rise of a generation of young men, themselves abandoned by society, who feel little responsibility for their progeny. The psychological neglect is compounded by economics. Fifty-five percent of kids in single-parent households live in poverty, Senator Moynihan writes, and they constitute the core of the 500,000 children who go to sleep homeless every night, the one in four kids who have dropped out of high school, and the ten million kids without any health insurance. Ultimate casualties of family disintegration and of the broader wilding culture and economic policies at its source, the worst off of these kids are called by *Newsweek* "American untouchables," reflecting a journalist's reaction to the sight and smell of filthy, impoverished infants and his feelings of shame at "resisting the affections of a tiny child whose entire being seems to emanate pathology." The plight of these victimized children should not obscure the struggles of one-parent kids at every income level. Many do not live in poverty but live disrupted lives, like Andy, aged eleven, cited in *Newsweek*, who was removed from his mother when she became abusive. He went to live with his aunt, but when her residence was being sold and she could not bring Andy to her next home, it was left unclear where he would live next.[27]

Within the two-parent household, and at the higher income levels, the larger wilding culture may be leading to a more invisible emotional sabotage of the family and abandonment of children. *Newsweek* opened its special issue on the family with a critique of affluent professionals who prize their careers or BMWs more than their children. The fact that many upper-middle-class young people are taking longer to get degrees, are flitting across careers, and are waiting longer before getting married and less time to get divorced, suggests that they find it increasingly difficult to make, in sociologist David Popenoe's words, a "commitment of any kind." This may reflect aborted emotional relations with professional parents too consumed by their own career drives to invest time in their kids. Many such kids get expensive stereos and cars instead of love, and while most expect to get married and have kids, "The prospect fills them with dread." Summarizing research findings, Kennth L.

Woodward maintains that they appear to constitute a generation that has "grown accustomed to keeping their options open. There are so many choices to make — in relationships, careers, and consumer goods — that they hate to limit their freedom." Many of these young people, beginning to suffer from their inability to make commitments, are flocking to codependency groups, a rapidly proliferating self-help movement focusing on the emotional devastation wreaked in dysfunctional families, a condition now said to include as many as 90 percent of American families.[28]

Dr. Benjamin Spock, America's best-known "family doctor," sees a direct connection between the undoing of the family and the values of the Reagan-Bush era. "By far the most disturbing force in America today," Spock says, "is excessive competitiveness. It keeps people obsessed with their jobs and with personal advancement," at the expense of feelings for others. Spock argues that the effects on the family are devastating, since it destroys the ethos of kindness and care on which loving families depend. Spock puts his finger on the essential wilding drama of the current era: unmitigated self-interest inevitably means abandonment of the family and, ultimately, as among the Ik, all social commitments.[29]

Too Taxing a Commitment: The Abandonment of Society

"The limo from the Honolulu airport is a lumbering, battered Buick," writes journalist Tom Ashbrook, noting his first impressions after returning from a ten-year sojourn in Asia. "The doors don't close properly. The seats are stained and torn. The suspension is drooping, cockeyed. The music is mushy. The paint is extravagantly scarred. The passengers are fat." Images of Japan still in his mind, Ashbrook is deeply disturbed.[30]

In Honolulu, Ashbrook again records his impressions. "Hello Occident. Cracked highways, no service. Hotel is heavy on glitter and self-promotional hype, light on everything else. Construction quality shabby. Rusting metalwork. Cheap materials. . . . Rich next to poor. Slick by shabby. Twitchy bag ladies and a legless panhandler croaking 'Aloha.' . . . Korean cabdriver complains road repairs take ten times longer than in Seoul."[31]

"An American homecoming," Ashbrook groans, "is a journey into shades of disarray." It is downright "scary for a recent returnee." Ashbrook learns that his brother-in-law "sleeps with a large pistol in his nightstand and an alarm system that can track a burglar room by room." Turning on the radio, Ashbrook hears of "Los Angeles drivers taking potshots at one another on the freeway, American schoolchildren scoring at the bottom of the First World heap in key subjects. Drug lords reigning over urban fiefs, Alcoholics Anonymous and its ilk as a new religion. Wall Street sapping the economy." Fresh into his hotel, Ashbrook's son flicks on a Saturday morning cartoon; "Hey fella! This is America," booms the wisecracking voice of an animated hero. "I've got the right to not work any time I want."[32]

The comparison with Asia is too disheartening for Ashbook. "While veins of efficiency and competence feel ever-expanding in Asia, they appear to be contracting in the United States. Our cracked highways and rusting bridges seem physical reflections of falling standards, organization, simple care in the performance of jobs—of lost resolve." Ashbook concludes that a "returning American comes home with trepidation," hoping that his sense of the breakdown of America "is exaggerated, fearing that it might not be, subtly prepared to accept it as fact."[33]

Ashbrook is seeing the unmistakable signs of a breakdown in both the physical and social infrastructure necessary to keep a society together. America's physical infrastructure, its grid of roads, bridges, railways, ports, airports, sewer systems, and communication nodes, is in near terminal disrepair. This is no surprise to the folks in Covington, Tennessee, where a bridge over the Hatchie River collapsed, sending seven motorists to their death; nor to people in upstate New York, where the collapse of a bridge killed ten people. Nearly half of Massachusetts' 5,027 bridges are officially "substandard." Two-thirds of these are so badly broken down that they need to be replaced. Moreover, 70 percent of Massachusetts roads are rated "fair" or "poor." Almost everywhere "The nation's roads are crumbling . . . existing highways go unrepaired while new ones seldom advance beyond the blueprint stage. Forty percent of the nation's bridges have serious deficiencies. Airports, like highways, are strained beyond capacity, while potential mass transit options go unexplored. Water delivery systems are so antiquated that some cities still transport water through nineteenth-century wooden pipes." California Democratic representative Robert T. Matsui says "The problem is absolutely catastrophic," perhaps an understatement given the price tag of repair estimated at over $3 trillion, which is three times the size of the annual federal budget and more than the entire national debt. Rebuilding the national infrastructure, Massachusetts transportation secretary Frederick P. Salvucci says, "is the greatest public works challenge since the pyramids were built."[34]

As the physical infrastructure collapses, the "social infrastructure" is being starved, creating an emergency in the provision of affordable housing, jobs at a liveable wage, basic health care, education, and social services required to sustain the fabric of civilization. The crisis of affordable housing has now yielded "over three million homeless people," writes journalist Michael Albert, "who wander our backstreets eating out of garbage cans and sleeping under tattered newspapers in bedrooms shared with alley-rats." About 11 percent of American families have fallen through gaping holes in the "safety net" and are poor, partly reflecting the unpleasant reality of an economy in decline churning out a high proportion of extremely low-wage jobs: 44 percent of the new jobs created during the eighties pay less than $7,400 a year, which is 35 percent less than the poverty-level income for a family of four. Over 36 million

Americans have no health insurance. This includes one-fifth of all American children, contributing to America's life expectancy being lower and infant mortality rate higher than in all of the Western European countries and some Eastern European countries too. Meanwhile, the collapse of American public education is yielding an average American high school student who not only has difficulty locating France, Israel, or the United States itself on a map, but scores lower across the board than students in virtually all the other advanced industrialized countries. This is well understood by American parents who shun the public school system when they can afford to do so. An estimated nine out of ten Boston parents send their kids to parochial school or any place other than a Boston public school.[35]

This abject unraveling of the entire social fabric is the ultimate manifestation of the new wilding culture, an abandonment of society consciously engineered by the country's political leadership and passively endorsed by the majority of voters. The cost of maintaining and reconstructing its physical and social infrastructure is well within the reach of the world's still richest country. In what may be the greatest act of domestic policy wilding in this century, recent presidents, while continuing to pour billions into the Pentagon's coffers, have refused to support the public spending that would halt and reverse the crumbling infrastructure. This refusal is rationalized under the umbrella of "free market" ideology, to wit rolling back taxes, deficits, and "big government." In contrast, Western European countries such as Belgium, France, West Germany, and the Netherlands, less wealthy than the United States, have managed to preserve much of their social infrastructure by spending a substantially higher percentage of their GNP on health care, education, and a wide range of other social programs.[36]

"No new taxes" is the ultimate symbol of the new public policy wilding, a thirty-second sound bite powerful enough to catapult two presidents into the White House. Cynically fueled by

politicians, the "tax revolt" has created the political space leaders needed to defund society, while reflecting the war in American's hearts and minds between their commitments to society
and to themselves. Refusing taxes has become the respectable
political vehicle to lash out at and ultimately abandon both
government and society itself. Future historians may come to
view American leaders playing the tax revolt as a sequel to the
emperor playing his violin as Rome burned.

Viewed as the ultimate display of political wilding and social
abandonment, the tax drama is at its most acute and most revealing right now in the states. Squeezed by declining federal aid
and local revenues set in stone by angry property owners, state
governments all over the country, including Oregon, New
York, Illinois, New Jersey, Texas, Massachusetts, Nebraska,
Nevada, and California, are struggling for survival. Many are
enacting wilding scripts that evoke the images of the Ik murdering their own society, unwilling or unable to raise public funds
as the states bleed to death.

Massachusetts politics, 1990 style, became a Roman circus
of tax-cutters competing to see who can kick more of the
stuffing out of vital social services and land the final knock-out
blow to state government itself. Driven by tax-cutting fever
and a deficit of a billion-plus dollars, the Massachusetts legislature produced one budget proposal after another shredding
health, education, and highway programs in a state whose infrastructure is already at the breaking point. "In Massachusetts, the emergency medical system is hanging by a
thread just for day-to-day operations," says Kenneth Leary,
director of emergency medical services for the Massachusetts
Hospital Association. The state nonetheless eliminated the
$375,000 line item to fund the Centralized Medical Emergency
Direction, putting at risk all patients needing emergency ambulance service.

Among the fallouts of the 1991 proposed fiscal budget: the "almost sure" possibility of increased drownings, already up 50
percent the previous year, as the state trims its lifeguards by 50

percent; increased illness and death from the state's 123 toxic
dumps as the state lays off 25 percent of its public health staff
(although people are already drinking water, Environment
Secretary John DeVillars reported, that is "heavily laden with
chemicals"); increases in outbreaks of syphilis, measles, and
whooping cough as the state cuts back 40 percent of the staff at
its disease control center, including those who inspect food; a
"very, very grave danger" of increased deaths from more bridge
collapses, according to Metropolitan District Commissioner
Ilyas Bhatti, as the state cut its road and bridge repair budget
20 percent in 1990 and planned a 30 percent cut for 1991; the significant prospect of more elderly prematurely dying, according
to the *Boston Globe*, as people are "kicked out of nursing homes"
due to elimination of the state subsidy provided for over 2,000
residents, including Julie Normand, aged seventy-eight, who
says "Where can you go when you can't dress or undress alone,
can't comb your hair? I have no sister or brother or children,
no one who can take care of me"; increases in the state's already
inflated infant mortality rate as the state cut by 30 percent its
funds for food and health services for impoverished, pregnant
women; a third consecutive year of increased child abuse as the
state cancels its plans to hire seventy more child caseworkers;
and a "10 percent increase in serious accidents and a 10 percent
increase in highway deaths," according to Maj. Thomas
Kennedy, the State Police's top planning official, as the state
seeks to cut 300 to 375 state troopers.[37]

Unwilling to levy new taxes, the state is cannibalizing itself.
Acknowledging that he was cutting not just fat but nerve and
bone, retiring governor Michael Dukakis called his own 1991
spending plan a "doomsday budget."

The 1990 Massachusetts legislature, jolted by the Moody Investors Service's decision to drop Massachusetts' bonds to a
junk bond rating, the lowest in the country, finally proposed
new taxes. But with the election of a new Republican governor,
William Weld, a fundamentalist tax-cutter, the prospects for
new taxes evaporated. In Weld's new regime, the suicidal dis-

mantling of state government accelerated, threatening the viability of everything from the judicial and prison systems to city libraries. [38]

The tax revolt all over the country is an intimate, perhaps suicidal, wilding dance between leaders and voters. Politicians and business conservatives are orchestrating the dance, according to Bob Kuttner, student of California's "Prop 13" revolt, "channeling the raucous popular energy of the tax revolt into an orderly drive for systematic limitations on the welfare state and reductions in taxes on the well-to-do." The rich are using legitimate grievances by overtaxed home owners and working people to reduce their own obligation to society. This proved such a fortuitous political recipe for the affluent that it has become the Bible of the Republican Party, leading to howls of protest among Republican Congressmen when President Bush readjusted his "no new taxes" pledge. What has proved a guaranteed ticket to the White House for the Republicans (and increasingly a condition of reelection for cynical Congressional Democrats) may prove disastrous to society as a whole, for it is doubtful that a society can survive when those governing it become an accessory to its breakdown.[39]

Ordinary voters are, at minimum, being willingly seduced to dance. John Powers argues that "cafeteria-style government is on the rise in Massachusetts as more taxpayers believe that they need pay only for what they order. Yes for plowing, no for schools. Hold the bridge repairs." Powers believes that Massachusetts voters may be breaking faith with their Constitution, defined as "A social compact, by which the whole people covenants with each Citizen and each Citizen with the whole people." In the tax revolt each voter is for himself or herself. The elderly and childless couples vote against raising taxes for schools. The young are seeking to ration health care for the elderly. And the well-to-do are prepared to cut back social services for the poor because in their eyes they are wasteful and create dependency. "Whatever happened," Powers asks, "to the common good?"[40]

Suzanne Gordon, an Arlington, Massachusetts writer watching her neighbors acquiesce in the closing of one junior high school, two branch libraries, and the cutback of 30 percent of the city's work force, sees the emergence of the "No Cares Cohort"—a "vast group of professionals between the ages of about twenty-five and forty. A lot of them don't have children till they're older, so they don't have to worry about taking care of them. They're young and healthy, so the disastrous decline in our health care system doesn't affect them. If they're married or living with someone, they're probably co-workaholics. . . . They are as removed from the social contract as those minority kids the system has truly abandoned." Gordon concludes that "our town is crumbling" because these residents are content to "sit idly by," with many "sucked into a swirl of antigovernment, antihuman frenzy . . . The spirit of generosity seems to have been executed in Massachusetts, if not in the nation as a whole."[41]

Yet substantial majorities of taxpayers continue to tell pollsters they support earmarked spending for public universities, universal health care, and other specifically targeted social services, even as they vote against general tax increases, suggesting caution in proposing that voters have turned wholesale into mean-spirited Scrooges. Many Massachusetts voters say that they want to continue to help those truly in need but see government programs as a gigantic hoax and a waste, subsidizing bureaucrats rather than the poor. The public response is as much an attempt to deliver a swift kick to an overfed public bureaucracy as it is an abandonment of the needy.

My own interviews with about thirty Massachusetts voters suggest that suburbanites, affluent and geographically insulated from city life, most closely fit the "mean spirited" image. Many seem prepared to see the cities abandoned if their own comfortable lives can be preserved. The wilding ethos of the suburbs and the more affluent urban neighborhoods expresses itself less as a "frenzied, antihuman" rage than as an increasingly thick wall that makes the suffering of others emotionally tolerable. Most of the voters I interviewed believe that the larger society may be in danger of falling apart, but find, nonetheless, a remarkable capacity to enjoy their own lives. That a growing segment of the population is hell-bent on having a good time even as they recognize that the ship may be sinking, is one of the most telling marks of the new wilding culture.[42]

7

Beyond Wilding
Resurrecting Civil Society

An injury to one is the concern of all.
KNIGHTS OF LABOR MOTTO

THE WILDING EPIDEMIC has taken a devastating toll on America, but it has not permanently incapacitated it. Societies, like individuals, have powerful natural resistances and remarkable capacities to regenerate themselves. While Ik society died from the disease, America, always a resilient society, has far greater economic and cultural resources to halt the epidemic and recapture social health. To succeed, however, it will have to focus all its efforts on the task, which involves shoring up "civil society" at its very foundations.

Civil society is the underlying antidote to the wilding virus, involving a culture of love, morality, and trust that leads people to care for one another and for the larger community. A civil society's institutions nurture civic responsibility by providing incentives for people to act not just in their own interest but for the common good. Governments can provide a supportive framework, but a robust civil society cannot be legislated. Civil society must arise from the cooperation and moral sensibilities of ordinary people, who understand that their own fulfillment requires thriving communities and an intact society.

Reflections on civil society date back to Aristotle, but have been revived in modern times by the cataclysmic changes in Eastern Europe and the Soviet Union. The dictatorial governments ruling for decades in the name of Communism systematically undermined civil society, crushing all independent groups or communities that could resist their rule. As the people, already suffering from preexisting ethnic and nationalist conflicts, became increasingly atomized, unable to trust either their governments or their fellow citizens, a wilding culture emerged. It remained largely invisible, held in check by the all-powerful authorities. But after 1989, with the collapse of the Berlin Wall and the governments it symbolized, the wilding forces, suppressed for so many years, were now free to surface. An epidemic erupted in the form of revived antisemitism, with other ethnic and ultranationalist poisons spreading through the region. Moreover, after the initial revolutionary euphoria had worn off, civic indifference, apathy, and a lack of trust and cooperation developed among citizens. Calls for the resurrection of civil society have reverberated from Budapest and Prague to Moscow, with some leaders, such as Czechoslovakian president Vaclav Havel, recognizing that the biggest challenge, ironically after decades of rule under the rhetoric of collectivism, is the rebuilding of community.

The wilding epidemics in Eastern Europe and the United States are different from one another; one was bred by coercive collectivism and the other by untrammeled free market individualism. Sociologist Alan Wolfe writes that both an overreaching government and an overblown market can, in different ways, colonize civil society and destroy it—the market, by glorifying selfishness, and the state, by substituting paternalism or coercion for conscience. Civil society blooms only where markets and governments are kept in reasonable check, and families, communities, and voluntary associations, the institutional seedbeds of love, morality, and trust, are free to prosper. The bonds of conscience and caring, as well as mechanisms of social accountability to be discussed below, help to ensure that private interests do not override the common good.[1]

While there is no magic formula and no perfect model, civil society, in the United States as well as Eastern Europe, is the strongest and most suitable medicine for the wilding epidemic.

Americans now urgently must recognize, as do virtually all Eastern Europeans, that they must dedicate themselves unwaveringly to reconstructing their society. America desperately needs its own perestroika. There are staggering obstacles, including the self-serving denials by many American leaders that a real domestic crisis exists. But if Americans can see through such happy-hour rhetoric, there are many reasons to believe that they can succeed.

The Case for Hope

Over one hundred years ago, Alexis de Tocqueville worried that America was vulnerable to an individualism that "saps the virtues of public life," and "in the long run" might "attack and destroy" society itself. Tocqueville described it as an individualism "which disposes each member of the community to sever himself from the mass of his fellows," and to "feel no longer bound by a common interest." Americans must always be on guard, Tocqueville advises, against the deterioration of their individualistic culture into "a passionate and exaggerated love of self, which leads a man to connect everything with himself, and to prefer himself to everything else in the world."[2]

Tocqueville did not disapprove of the healthy self-interest that energized Americans, but he saw the thin line separating American individualism from wilding. Without strongly developed moral codes, the restless pursuit of self-interest bred in a market economy could at any time degrade into an egoistic cancer that would destroy society. But Tocqueville, a sober observer, was also extraordinarily optimistic about the American experiment. Counteracting the wilding virus was another side of America, the strength of its civil society. One manifestation was the personal generosity and helpfulness that he observed in all his American travels. "Although private interest directs the greater part of human actions in the United States," Tocqueville wrote, " it does not regulate them all. I must say that

I have often seen Americans make great and real sacrifices to the public welfare; and I have remarked a hundred instances in which they hardly ever failed to lend faithful support to each other." Because an American is never master nor slave of his fellow creature, "his heart readily leans to the side of kindness."[3]

Tocqueville recognized that the kinder and gentler side of American life was grounded in the political rights and free institutions which "remind every citizen, and in a thousand ways, that he lives in society." Tocqueville marveled at the American propensity to "constantly form associations" of a thousand kinds where they "voluntarily learn to help each other." Americans were constantly connecting and spontaneously creating bonds of friendship, trust, and cooperation that lie at the heart of civil society.[4]

In the 150 years since Tocqueville's visit, the wilding epidemic has spread throughout America, but it has not totally destroyed the civil society that made such an impression on him. Much evidence suggests that Americans retain some of the openness, generosity, and moral idealism that, in Tocqueville's view, differentiated them from Europeans. Likewise, the free institutions and "propensity to associate" have not vanished. It is the sturdiness of this base, its survival in the face of the wilding onslaught, that offers grounds for optimism and a direction for the future.

While wilding stories make sensational copy and fill the newspapers, there are also plenty of stories testifying to the survival of the side of the American heart "that readily leans toward kindness." On May 15, 1991, next to a story about the drug-related murder of an entire family, the *New York Times* reported that a woman fell six stories to her death while trying to rescue a friend's child. To reach the child, trapped near the top of a West Side hotel, she had secured a sturdy television cable around her waist, tied the other end to a pipe, and tried to lower herself from the roof. The cable broke and she fell sixty feet. The woman, Jackie Knight, aged thirty-one, was a former foster child and had a child of her own.[5]

Each year in Boston, where stray bullets now terrorize whole neighborhoods, a remarkable number of people, 40,000 in 1990, join the Walk for Hunger. The marchers hike for twenty miles, often in inclement weather, to raise money for Project Bread, a group that helps provide meals for the homeless and hungry. Each participant takes time to approach "sponsors," who agree to donate a certain amount of money for each mile that the walker completes. In 1990, marchers collected $4 million in pledges. As one curbside viewer said, "You've got the elderly walking, you've got kids walking, you've got families walking. To me, it's the most beautiful sight to see all the people walking." Such walks are only one of a cornucopia of charitable endeavors that take place in cities and towns across the United States.

At the very time that taxpayers are revolting and turning off the public spigot, volunteers are stepping in to help stop the bleeding that their own votes have precipitated. In many towns across the country, playground construction is done mainly by volunteers, in the spirit of traditional community barn-raising. In Plymouth, Massachusetts, the town library stays open only because of the generosity of over fifty volunteers; in nearby Raynham, the school libraries are run entirely by volunteers. Community booster groups rally to raise money to keep public buildings painted, keep school sports programs going, and plant trees and maintain the city parks.[6]

Even in the heart of Wall Street there are signs of the other America. In 1987, several multimillionaire commodities traders created Robin Hood Foundation, an off-beat center that scours New York City "looking for neighborhood foundations that rescue the homeless, care for children with AIDS, fight drug abuse or rebuild families." The organization raised over $2 million in 1990, and seeks to link community activists to business sponsors or technical experts that can be helpful. One of the founders says, "I couldn't sleep if I did not have a part in this sort of thing," and another says, "I love this city with a passion. I'm a walking poster for New York. I don't want to see the city go under."[7]

Such anecdotes are backed up by hard statistics documenting the generous side of America. A Gallup poll found in 1987 that more than seven of every ten households contribute to charity, donating an average of $790 or almost 2 percent of household income, a figure almost four times greater than that in Canada and England (a comparison that should take into account the national health plans and large social welfare programs that taxpayers in the latter countries support, thereby reducing the need for charity). Also in 1987, 80 million Americans over age eighteen, about 45 percent of the national population over that age, sacrificed their own time to volunteer, on average about 4.7 hours a week, totalling almost 20 billion hours of volunteer time in the country. This represents a slight decline from 1981, mostly accounted for by reductions in volunteering among the group aged eighteen to twenty-four. But the total contribution remains impressive, including, in 1987, over 153 million individual contributions to charity and an estimated 194 million volunteer assignments carried out. Over 75 percent of the population say they have an obligation to help others, indicating the persistence of moral currents in the country during the peak Reagan years, although only approximately half of these follow through and volunteer.[8]

How can the wilding epidemic spread at the same time that moral commitments and compassionate behavior persist at these levels? As I argued in Chapter 1, America in the 1990s is host simultaneously to a wilding culture and a civic culture, with sectors of the elites increasingly immersed in wilding and a vast number of ordinary Americans uneasily straddling the two cultures. Most Americans' lives are a struggle to reconcile wilding impulses with a nagging conscience that refuses to die. Many succumb to wilding pressures at the office but rediscover their humanity with family or friends. Conversely, some become wilders in personal life but express their conscience in admirable careers dedicated to constructive professional or business enterprise, public service, or social change.

The stubborn persistence of civil society and moral commitment provides a fertile seedbed for social reconstruction. The way to stop the wilding epidemic is to bolster all the empathic and moral sensibilities that Americans already display. While these need to be fortified and mobilized with new visions, the project is more akin to catalyzing the surviving immune system of a weakened patient than seeking to transplant a new immune system to the patient whose own defenses have been destroyed.

But stopping the epidemic will take serious cultural and institutional change. As I have argued, the wilding epidemic grows out of an American individualism that is deeply rooted. America's leadership and major institutions increasingly fuel Americans' wilding side and provide serious disincentives to their less egoistic inclinations. We need the culture, economics, and politics of a civil society, where the rules of the success game encourage attention to morality and the common good. More precisely, we must rewrite the rules of the game such that those who neglect the collective interest will not prosper, while those who take it into account will realize their just rewards.

Rethinking the American Dream: The Culture of Civil Society

The American Dream has not always been a cultural template for the wilding virus. As we consider rewriting the dream for a better future, we have the consolation that we can look to our history for guidance. Through most of the American past, the purely materialistic and individualistic side of the dream has been balanced by a moral and community-oriented side, preventing the dream from transmuting into a wilding recipe. Moreover, the dream has been inclusive, defining a set of common purposes to which all Americans could aspire. These historical features of the dream need to be recaptured in order to fortify civil society and purge the wilding epidemic.

The individualistic dream dominating today has its roots in the mythology of "self-made men" and, as James Combs argues, "stems from the ideology of capitalism and the myth of unlimited abundance." As noted in Chapter 3, the nineteenth-century novelist Horatio Alger immortalized the materialist dream in his "rags to riches" fables. In its current form, it celebrates American heroes like the basketball superstar Michael Jordan, who rose to fabulous success by extraordinary individual talent and hard work.[9]

The materialistic dimensions of the dream have become so dominant that most Americans have forgotten there once was another side to the dream. America has traditionally defined itself in terms of a set of high moral ideals, including democracy, equality, and tolerance. Values growing out of the religious and political foundations of the country, including the Puritan zeal for community and the American Revolution's idealization of civic democracy, helped to shape another dream, one that mythologized family, community, and civic responsibility. Through most of American history, the materialistic dream prevailed, but the dream that elevated community values warned that success should not be achieved at any price. America idealized its rural and small town communities where, to a greater or lesser degree, as Combs notes, "religion, family, and democratic good feelings tempered the quest for power and money."[10]

The two dreams define a creative tension in America's history. In the 1930s, the Great Depression mobilized Americans to rally together and fashion a collective lifeline to ride out the economic storm. President Franklin Delano Roosevelt reinvigorated the dream of moral community, using the government to affirm that in a time of desperate need, Americans would take care of each other. Three decades later, in the 1960s, a whole generation of youth plunged into social activism and communal experiments, seeking a morally attractive alternative to the materialist dream of their 1950s childhoods.

The failure of the aspirations of the sixties led, in the seventies and eighties, to perhaps the most thorough-going subordination of the moral dream in American history. Of the presidents since the sixties, only President Carter, inept and unsuccessful, sought to revive the moral quest. But to purge the wilding epidemic, Americans in the 1990s will have to rediscover and refashion a version of the moral dream that can temper the current fever of individualistic materialism and resurrect civil society.

The moral vision will have to be creative, in keeping with the new threats that unchecked materialism now pose. It will have to encompass an ecological morality, for we now know that the untrammeled materialist dream is incompatible with planetary survival, becoming a form of wilding directed against nature itself. The Greenhouse Effect, the catastrophic heating up of the earth through promiscuous use of fossil fuels, is only the most frightening of the legacies of such environmental wilding. If Americans cannot learn to live within the limits dictated by the environment, they will be engaged not only in crimes against nature, but in a form of wilding against future generations who will bear the ultimate consequences.

Americans find it hard to accept any limits on materialism, for the dominant dream has equated freedom and fulfillment with the right to get as rich or famous as luck, talent, or hard work permits. To suggest that Michael Milken should not have been allowed to make or keep the $550 million he made in 1987 has an un-American ring. But a civil society must respect not only ecological limits but also those dictated by the traditional American morality of fair play and egalitarianism. Uncapping all limits in the recent orgy of greed and deregulation has untenably polarized the country, creating, as Kevin Phillips writes, an unprecedented and morally unbearable division between rich and poor.[11]

Civil society is a society of inclusion, and the new dream will have to script new trade-offs between individual freedom and the survival of the community. This ultimately requires reviving a moral dream of community, not the utopian vision of communes that failed in the 1960s, but something simultaneously more modest and more ambitious: the reawakening of the American sense of community that can mobilize the country to unify and preserve itself in an era of unprecedented division.

Today, when the wilding epidemic has placed the survival of society itself in jeopardy, the new dream has to focus Americans on the common task of saving their society. Ironically, as suggested above, Americans have been led by their present leaders into thinking about "saving" every society but their own. President John Adams in the eighteenth century said that America should try to help other nations but "should go not abroad seeking monsters to destroy." Such common sense is reinforced when there are real dragons at home to slay. James Reston, the senior *New York Times* political commentator, writes that rather than dreaming of a "new world order," we should be urgently dedicating ourselves to "a new American order" at home.[12]

As the world shrinks, Americans may be influenced by examples of civil society abroad, especially those of new global winners, such as Japan. Japan has sensational financial and political scandals of its own, but has preserved its social infrastructure and is far less plagued by wilding. There is little crime in the streets of Tokyo or Osaka and the Japanese family is intact; indeed, the entire society maintains the sensibility of one extended family. Although Americans are hardly likely to embrace the Japanese model, the Japanese economic miracle may jolt Americans into the recognition that tilting the balance back toward community is not only essential for survival but a recipe for success.

While the Japanese are passionate baseball fans and avid consumers of Steve's ice cream and Big Macs, they are anything but converts to the American Dream. Michio Morishima, seeking to answer the question, "Why has Japan succeeded?" observes that beneath the glittering Western facade, Japanese culture remains profoundly shaped by Confucianism. A deeply nonindividualistic philosophy, Confucianism holds up the love of the group rather than the success of the individual as the highest virtue. Only "when the natural human affection found within the family was extended absolutely freely beyond the confines of the family, both to nonfamily members and to complete strangers," Confucius believed, could human nature reach "perfection and the social order [be] appropriately maintained." Japanese corporations remain as much Confucian as capitalist, thriving on the loyalty of employees who view the company as their second family. The entire Japanese economy is a Confucian market that Adam Smith might not recognize, since everyone acts to benefit not so much themselves as their companies and communities and to solidify their connections to them.[13]

Americans do not have to embrace Confucianism to recognize that the country needs to strike a better balance between the individual and the group, both to survive as a civil society and to prosper in the world economy. Such a profound cultural shift, however, will happen slowly and arise as much from a reinterpretation of America's own experience as from any influences abroad. America's love affair with sports is only one of many areas where Americans already understand, without fully appreciating the implication of their own knowledge, that success is a team effort. The case of Michael Jordan is instructive. Polls in 1991 showed Jordan, after he led the Chicago Bulls to the National Basketball Association world title, as one of the five best-known and most admired figures in America. The public assimilated Jordan into the heroic tradition of the individualistic dream, a man who literally soared to fame and fortune through his own efforts. But the fans knew that the real lesson of Jordan and the Bulls was that winning comes only when the individual, no matter how extraordinary, subordinates his own game to the team effort.

Jordan was the Michael Milken of professional basketball, piling up points as fast as Milken accumulated junk bonds. He led the league in scoring for five years running, awing fans and players alike with the most graceful and dazzling moves ever seen on the courts. But it was a one-man show and his teammates seemed unable to muster the spirit to win.

By 1990, Jordan and his team had worked out a new social contract. Jordan would still be the prime mover, but he would concentrate more on opening up opportunities for his teammates. He would drive to the center or one side, and when double-teamed or triple-teamed, he would whip the ball back to one of his open teammates. Jordan became as good a passer as a scorer and fully integrated his team into the offense. When the Bulls won the championship in 1991, the secret was not Jordan's pyrotechnics, still dazzling as ever, but the new team chemistry. In the final championship series, there was one game where the Bulls seemed to slip back into their old way, with Jordan carrying the whole offense. Jordan never allowed that to recur, taking hardly any shots in the first quarter of the game that followed to ensure that his teammates got into the game early. Jordan's "sacrifice" brought his team victory and greater glory than he ever could achieve on his own.

Jordan fully understood that the victory was the team's, not his own. After the championship series, the individual selected as Most Valuable Player is touted each year in a Disney commercial. Jordan refused to do the commercial unless the recognition, including the money, was extended to the whole team. In what should be a symbol for America in the 1990s, the camera showed not a lone triumphant Michael Jordan, but a Jordan embracing his teammates, celebrating the Bulls as a winning family.

America needs to rewrite its social contract in the Jordan spirit. The culture of civil society is one of cooperation, invoking equal respect for the rights of individuals and the needs of the collective. Americans already intuitively recognize that the community has its own legitimate claims, responding positively a generation ago to John F. Kennedy's call to "Ask not what your country can do for you, but what you can do for your country." As civil society disintegrates, Americans need to ponder seriously such rhetoric and translate it into a new way of life. This will require a rewrite of the American Dream and an initially painful acceptance of limits on individual self-aggrandizement. But as the Jordan case suggests, such restraints on the self will ultimately serve the collectivity and each self within it.

Rescripting the American Dream will demand a recharging of American cultural institutions responsible for moral development, especially schools, churches, and families. Unfortunately, wilding culture has already taken a deadly toll on these institutions, and the public debate about reviving them has been dominated by well-heeled groups who seek mainly to buttress free market morality. Yet, as sociologist Amitai Etzioni argues, these are the key institutions that can "serve to countervail excessive individualism," and they will have to rediscover a moral compass counteracting the market ethos of their host culture.[14]

Much will depend on the courage of intellectuals, teachers, and clerics, who have to be uncompromising in teaching that the ethos of fast money, careerism, and obsessional self-aggrandizement spells death for society, while also helping Americans articulate their hunger for community and their vision of the common good. Intellectuals will have to overcome the pressures to conform and show, by their personal example as well as their writings and preachings, that "making it" is not the ultimate value. Institutional change will challenge the moral fiber of both teachers and academic administrators. New financial pressures, for example, are making universities ever more dependent on corporate funding, while many elementary schools will soon be operated as profit-making private enterprises. This threatens to turn American education into the chattel of its corporate class, reinforcing the unpublicized "PC" or politically correct dogma of mainstream American economic thinking and making it ever more difficult to teach a morality that transcends the market. Education leaders must act now to ensure that schools and universities resist the changes that will compromise their moral mission, insisting on institutional arrangements that prevent the collapse of the pursuit of knowledge into the pursuit of profit. Some promising beginnings have emerged in the tattered public school system in Chicago, where efforts have been made to revive public education through new forms of parental involvement and community control, tentatively shaking up the entrenched bureaucracy and drawing on the fresh energies and ideas of those with the biggest stake: parents, teachers, and the kids themselves.

The Social Market: The Economics of Civil Society

On June 12, 1991, President Bush, while pondering a new domestic strategy for the 1992 elections, made a stunning public confession that "the free market had failed." To solve domestic problems in the 1980s, "conventional wisdom turned to the genius of the free market," the president explained. "We began a decade of exceptional economic growth and created 20 million new jobs. And yet, let's face it, many of our streets are still not safe, our schools have lost their edge, and millions still trudge the path of poverty." This remarkable statement, something akin to the pope publicly renouncing Catholicism, was a frank acknowledgement of the incompatibilities between the free market and civil society.

Political pundits and the public rapidly discounted the president's statement, since he did not follow it up with any new policy initiatives. But it was significant not only because of the source of the remark, but because it reflected nagging doubts about the free market that have persisted through much of American history. As Americans have struggled to choose between the materialist dream and the moral dream, they have had to wrestle with the tensions between the free market and community. The market system was an excellent vehicle for delivering the promises of the materialist dream, but as Bush himself finally seemed to recognize, it was far less effective in preserving the moral fiber of society. In periods like the 1930s and 1960s, when the moral dream has come more strongly to the fore, Americans have pioneered economic models, like the New Deal, that depart from the free market scripture.

When Bush delivered his speech on free market failure, he said that there was a "better way," suggesting that to "tackle the urgent problems on the home front" required new economic thinking. Unfortunately, virtually the only innovative economics in his administration has been by those zealots who seek to have the market take over everything from the public schools to police protection. Some advocate such innovations as a perfect "free market in babies," which could help resolve the abortion debate by making it "economically feasible for (especially poor) mothers to carry their babies to term and then sell them." Such radical extensions of the market model, exemplified by surrogate parenting, help to highlight the ways in which the free market violates civil society. Surrogate mother Mary Beth Whitehead sued to get her baby back, feeling she was wilding against her own humanity by selling her infant. In the pure free market, as Gary Becker, one of its leading intellectual advocates, proposes, the cash nexus governs "all human behavior," including relations between teachers and students, men and women, parents and children. One does not have to be a fan of Karl Marx to recognize that such commodification of life undermines the trust, love, and morality that sustains civil society.[15]

In the wake of Communism's collapse, the Bush administration tried to export its free market revolution abroad rather than find pro-social economic alternatives at home. But the Eastern Europeans are paying more attention to their fellow Europeans, especially the West Germans, who long ago renounced the free market model and embraced what they now call "the social market." The attraction is that they have not only prospered economically, but, like the Japanese, have preserved civil society and maintained, until the stresses of reunification caused a recent explosion of attacks on immigrants, an impressive immunity from the wilding epidemic. As Helmut Giesecke, head of the foreign trade department in the Association of German Chambers of Industry and Commerce, asks, "Do you see people on the street here? Are they without cars? They have decent food, housing and clothes, and their children are well educated." He is polite enough not to mention that the murder rate in his country is barely one-tenth that in America, although this will come as no surprise to most American tourists, who feel safer on the streets of Frankfurt or Bonn than Detroit or New York.[16]

This is the legacy of a century of European efforts to build an alternative with a social conscience to the free market. The Swedes, Danes, Austrians, and Germans recognize that they are not playing Adam Smith's game. "We are not operating a marketplace economy," admits German industrialist Giesecke, but rather a "social marketplace economy," that "guarantees food, shelter, schooling, and medical attention to every person, not as welfare but as human rights." Government, labor, and business work together to reconcile prosperity with social justice. German business has supported this program, according to Giesecke, because "this social network really works," leading to a well-educated, healthy, and motivated work force whose productivity keeps increasing.[17]

Perhaps ultimately the Germans support the social infrastructure because they know firsthand the horrific consequences when society totally breaks down. They have experienced a Germany gone completely wild, and many recognize it could happen again. The greater internal homogeneity of Germany, Austria, Sweden, and other European "social market" societies also allows them to feel a greater connection to others and savor the sense of "we are family" so powerful in Japan. Even as European cultures grow more individualistic and consumerist, their social marketplace economies may prevent a descent into wilding.

The development of an American social market could be one of the most potent remedies for the wilding epidemic. It suggests a way to reconcile economic growth and justice, and to help solve America's social problems by building on its own deepest value: democracy. It is potentially the basis for an American perestroika.

The social market is the economic recipe for a civil society, but the Western European version is not the one Americans are likely to embrace. The European model is a universal welfare state, in which the government shelters groups unprotected by the market, responds to medical, housing, and social needs of the population that the market neglects, and comprehensively regulates business to ensure social responsibility. But American history, as well as its current fiscal crisis, militates against the likelihood that Americans, barring another Great Depression, will look to the state. While there is a crucial role for government to play in stopping the wilding epidemic, it can only be a catalyst, not the central player.

The key to a social market system is not big government but new institutions, whether public or private, that rectify the tendency of our current market economy to write social costs and benefits out of the equation. The American free market responds mainly to the desires of the individual and is largely indifferent to the spillover effects that transactions have on the rest of society. When a factory decides to pollute, the social cost of bad air and ensuing discomfort or respiratory diseases is what economists call an "externality," a real cost but one that the owner can ignore, since it is society rather than the factory that pays the ultimate bill. In the pure free market model, there is no economic incentive for the individual to help society nor any market disincentive to be antisocial; the market simply does not discriminate, operating with what passes as "benign neglect." As such neglect accumulates, with the market turning a blind eye to the millions of "externalities" that affect society every day, benign neglect becomes catastrophic social blindness and civil society is placed in jeopardy.

A social market corrects such social blindness by writing social costs and benefits back into the equation. It is a market that seeks to "internalize" the externalities and thus become socially responsible, by giving social stakeholders a voice in corporate decisions and by devising strategies to guarantee that the economic wilder will pay a cost for his sociopathic behavior (and, conversely, that the good citizen will get his or her just rewards). One way to do this is to rely on government, which can compel prosocial choices by legislation or induce them through tax incentives, as when the state enforces worker health and safety standards or gives tax credits to factories installing antipollution devices. But there is another tack, one appetizing to Americans wary of government and committed to democracy, which involves redesigning economic institutions to be better equipped to exercise social responsibility on their own initiative. One such approach is new corporate ownership and participation arrangements, where workers or local citizens gain a voice and can speak up for the needs of the larger community. The West Germans, while relying mainly on government, also have invented a "codetermination" system, which requires that every industrial enterprise with more than 500 workers select half its governing board of trustees from among its own employees. This has been successful for over forty years, contributing not only to the German economic boom, but to a civil industrial society in which ordinary workers have been able to ensure that their health and safety are protected, their grievances addressed, and their jobs protected by investment strategies that prioritize domestic employment as well as overseas profit. Codetermination is a version of "economic democracy" that works.

In a series of seminal books, sociologist Severyn Bruyn describes the many down-to-earth ways, some already highly developed in America, to fashion a self-regulating social market, that is, one that works to dissuade economic wilding and preserve civil society without resorting to big government. Numerous forms of worker ownership and participation, including cooperatives and employee stock ownership plans (ESOPs) in which employees own a piece or all of their companies, can help compel the company to treat its employees fairly and practice workplace democracy. The cooperative, as its name implies, has the potential to turn the workplace into a civil society, since everyone in it has equal rights and self-interest is more closely wedded to the collective interest than in a conventional firm. Another innovation is corporate social charters that bind businesses to serve designated social missions, as in the case of community credit unions that are structured to reinvest in the community and offer low-interest loans to poorer residents. Land trusts, modern versions of the colonial concept of the "commons," can remove property from the commercial market and legally ensure that it serves community needs. A new field of social accounting can help take stock of the social costs and benefits of corporate decisions. "Social capital," such as the over $1 trillion in American pension funds, one of the largest, and still growing, pots of money in the world, can be used to invest in affordable housing and community economic development. A new practice of "social investing" could be the first step in turning the stock market into what sociologist Ritchie Lowry calls "good money," where investors seek a profit but also a social return on their money. "Social screens"—report cards on companies compiled by outside analysts—now tell investors which corporations are economic wilders and which good citizens. Companies seeking to attract the funds of millions of "social investors" have to demonstrate not only what they are doing for the bottom line, but what they are doing for their communities.[18]

America has not yet built a main highway toward this version of the social market, but it is already carving out many smaller roads in that direction. There are now over 10,000 American ESOPs, including huge companies like Avis Rent-a-Car and Weirton Steel, and there is evidence that they are more responsive to their employees and their customers. Studies show that worker owners are more productive and deliver high quality, with Avis now number one in ratings of customer satisfaction. Hundreds of ESOPs and cooperatives, including large worker-owned factories, practice sophisticated forms of workplace democracy. They are proving effective in job creation and retention, and are responsible for saving hundreds of jobs during the epidemic of factory closings in the last decade. According to polls, including one by Peter Hart in the late 1980s, "economic democracy" makes sense to most Americans; approximately 70 percent say that they would welcome the opportunity to work in an employee-owned company.[19]

By 1985, there were already over 500 land trusts nationwide, which have since helped rehabilitate inner-city neighborhoods as well as preserve rural acreage. Pension funds, such as those of state and municipal employees in California and New York, have already invested hundreds of millions of dollars in affordable housing and community economic development. Lowry estimates that American "social investors" have plowed somewhere between half a trillion and a trillion dollars into "ethical investments," rewarding corporations such as Ben and Jerry's, a highly profitable and socially progressive ice cream company. The company buys nuts harvested from the threatened Brazilian rain forests and gives almost half the profits to organizations fighting to save the forests; it also keeps an extremely low ratio of five to one between its highest and lowest paid employees, cultivating a spirit of egalitarianism that pays off in happier and more motivated employees.[20]

The political genius of these social market innovations is that they are attractive to liberals, because they promote equality and justice, as well as to conservatives, since they do not require massive government intervention and offer ordinary citizens a greater stake in the marketplace. In the 1970s Senator Russell Long, a conservative Democrat from Louisiana, was the prime sponsor in the Senate for employee ownership legislation, and the idea found considerable support in the Reagan White House as a strategy for building "people's capitalism." Liberal activists in universities, unions, and local communities, also fight for employee ownership, as a way to save jobs and increase workers' control.

Any idea that can draw such enthusiastic support from both sides of the political spectrum has the potential to be instituted on a large scale. At the same time, most of the more radical social market innovations have been resisted by powerful forces, as in the case of banks systematically denying credit to cooperatives. Mainstream business and politicians have also worked to water down innovations such as ESOPs to keep them from turning real decision-making power over to workers. Nonetheless, both political parties, and particulary those Democrats who criticize the black hole of domestic policy in the administration and seek real solutions to America's crisis, should hone the idea of the social market as a new public philosophy and the basis of a legislative agenda that would provide a decisive answer to "Where's the Beef?"— the campaign stopper that undermined Democrat Gary Hart's 1984 run for the presidency.

While government is not the prime mover in this emerging social market, it has helped midwife the new system and will have to nurture it further if it is to grow and become preservative of civil society. Government has to set up the legislative framework for corporate social charters, ESOPs, and worker cooperatives, establish the legal safeguards and guidelines for social investment of pension funds, provide encouragement through loans and tax credits for employee ownership and community development funds, and help oversee and underwrite the entire new economic nexus. Its regulatory role will remain powerful for many years and will never disappear, for, as we suggest below, many public interests can only be guaranteed by the state. But unlike communism or socialism, the government does not give the marching orders or own the means of production; the social market is still a market system, infused with Confucian sensibilities.

In the context of the current wilding crisis, government also has a more urgent short-term agenda. Saving civil society cannot wait until the full blossoming of the social market, and government will have to act in the interim to shore up the social foundations. This will require a version of the Marshall Plan for domestic reconstruction, but it will not bankrupt the economy or plunge the country into another Great Depression; in fact, as economist John Kenneth Galbraith observes, as "governments are tightening budgets, curtailing services, reducing payrolls, furloughing workers," they are only aggravating recessionary forces and by changing course, could help pull the country out of its doldrums. Galbraith proposes that government finance, by new borrowing if necessary, a modern day Reconstruction Finance Corporation charged with the immediate task of trying to plug the biggest holes in the country's physical and social infrastructure. As far as the latter is concerned, the costs might not be as large as some fear. A leading social policy analyst suggests that the cost of all social programs necessary to rehabilitate the inner cities is between $10 billion and $25 billion a year, less than one-thirtieth of the federal budget and cheaper than a squadron of Stealth bombers.[21]

There is special urgency now regarding children, for governmental inaction threatens to guarantee that the next generation will mature into uninhibited wilders. As civil society unravels, children are the most vulnerable group, being totally dependent on the love, moral guidance, and social spending that are casualties of the wilding culture. The state cannot raise and socialize children, but one of its highest priorities should be to help finance and save institutions, including the family and schools, that have to do the job. These are now in such a desperate condition that further "benign neglect" is unacceptable; moreover, sensible and economical family and educational strategies have already been articulated by numerous national commissions and children's advocates, such as the Children's Defense Fund. The Fund argues that it would only take about $20 billion a year to bail children and families out of poverty, a fraction of what Congress has already appropriated to bail out the S and Ls. None of these programs are utopian and none need to be budget-busters; coalitions of grass-roots groups have already mobilized to try to push them through a recalcitrant Congress and an even more recalcitrant White House.

The rise of the embryonic social market is part of a second American revolution, this one for economic rights and to save the society liberated by the Revolution two hundred years ago. Then, the issue was inventing a political constitution; now it involves rewriting the economic constitution. As in the first Revolution, ordinary citizens will have to struggle against powerful entrenched forces, the King Georges of contemporary America who are more dedicated to their own privileges than saving civil society in America.

A New Bill of Rights? The Politics of Civil Society

America's romance with individualism and the free market has its virtues, but it has clouded Americans' understanding of what makes society tick. Civil society arises only when people develop strong obligations to the larger "us" that can override the perennial, very human preoccupation with "me, me, me." Such larger commitments bloom only under special conditions, when the community shows that it cares so deeply for each of its members that each, in turn, fully understands his debt to society and seeks to pay it back in full.

The Japanese and Europeans, in their very different ways, seem to appreciate this "deal" or contract that preserves civil society. The Japanese corporation smothers the Japanese worker in a cocoon of secure employment, health benefits, housing, and other social necessities that make it almost impossible for workers to imagine life outside of the group. Through their expansive welfare states, the Europeans deliver their own bushel of benefits and entitlements that the citizen recognizes as indispensable to personal survival and happiness. Both systems bring their own serious problems, but succeed in creating the allegiance to the larger community that breeds immunity to the wilding epidemic.

Each civil society has to find its own way of inspiring its members' devotion, but all must deliver those rock bottom necessities essential to the pursuit of life, liberty, and happiness. These include a minimal level of personal safety, food, shelter, and a livelihood. "Social orphans" deprived of these essentials are unable to fulfill any larger obligation to society, for their existence is entirely consumed by the brutish struggle for personal survival.

This leads to the idea of "social citizenship," an extension of the familiar but narrower concept of political citizenship. The rights to health care, housing, and a job can be seen as social rights, parallel to our political rights to vote and to free speech enshrined in our constitution. Political rights apply to all citizens automatically, because they are the precondition of democracy as a system. Analogously, social rights should be extended automatically to everyone, for they are the precondition of civil society's survival.

The Japanese deliver such social rights through a paternalistic corporate extended family, largely private, while the Europeans do it through the welfare state. America will have to find its own way. Ideally, the emerging institutions of the social market would, in the long run, provide a local, democratic, and nonstatist solution. One possibility is an American version of the success achieved by Mondragon, a remarkable complex of over one hundred industrial cooperatives in the Basque region of Spain. Mondragon has succeeded during the past forty years in guaranteeing job security, housing, health care, and education to its members with scarcely any help from the state. Workers in the cooperatives have created cooperative schools, hospitals, insurance companies, and banks that offer robust social security from birth to death. The Mondragon complex, which is the largest manufacturer of durable goods in Spain and employs thousands of "worker-owners," has never permanently laid off a worker, reproducing the equivalent of the Japanese system of lifetime employment, while also entrepreneuring new cooperatives in one of the most impressive rates of job creation in the world.

Whether an American social market could evolve in such a direction is purely speculative, but clearly there are ways to provide social rights that are realistic, democratic, and do not require big government. America is the only major industrialized country not to offer health care as a social right to all its citizens. The problem could be easily rectified through a national health care system that is neither bureaucratic nor necessarily public. The 1990s has already seen the proliferation of a variety of proposals for privately financed national health care, relying on the existing network of health deliverers and insurers and largely financed by employers. More comprehensive publicly financed plans, including the Health USA Act of 1991 proposed by Nebraska senator Bob Kerrey, could simultaneously solve problems of cost and access without creating a huge government bureaucracy. Similarly, proposals abound for providing affordable housing in ways that integrate private and public financing mechanisms and do not make Uncle Sam everybody's landlord.[22]

While government is not the preferred agent, it is the guarantor of last resort. When people are homeless, starving, or jobless, civil society has failed, and a wilding virus is activated. It is not silly idealism or bleeding heart liberalism, but a conservative and prudent defense of the social order that requires public action.

For this reason, legal scholars like Columbia University law professor Louis Henkin are pointing to "genetic defects" in our Bill of Rights that constitutionally guarantee political but not social citizenship rights. Chief Justice William Rehnquist, in a 1989 court opinion, argued that the Constitution confers "no affirmative right to governmental aid, even when such aid may be necessary to secure life." This leads constitutional attorney Paul Savoy, former dean of John F. Kennedy University School of Law, to point out that "Our civil rights and civil liberties are rights in the negative sense" and "do not include affirmative obligations on government. We do not have a constitutional right," Savoy observes, "to have the state provide us with health care, or give us shelter if we are homeless, or prevent a child from being beaten or from starving to death." A coalition of unions, environmentalists, and community groups has responded by calling for a second Bill of Rights that would entitle all citizens to the elementary social rights of shelter, food, and health care.[23]

Social rights are not a free ride for the population, for with them come demanding social obligations. Citizenship is an intimate dance of rights and obligations, and "social citizens" need to embrace enthusiastically the moral obligations that come with their new entitlements. This means not only willingly paying the taxes required to keep civil society healthy, but also devoting time and effort, as we detail below, to "community-building" at work, in the neighborhood and in the country at large.

The problem with the Left is that it demands rights without spelling out the obligations that have to accompany them; the problem with the Right is that it expects obligations to be fulfilled without ceding social rights in return. Both positions are absurd, since rights and obligations are flip sides of civil society's coin of the realm. We need a new politics that marries the Left's moral passion for rights with the Right's sober recognition of duty.

Defending Our Lives: Getting from Here to There

But what do we do now? Americans are a pragmatic people and want down-to-earth answers. While there is no recipe or magic formula, we can act now to stop the wilding epidemic. If we want to survive with our humanity intact, we really have no alternative.

Since the wilding epidemic is a cancer that can destroy society, we are all patients fighting to stay alive. Obviously, if we each felt we had a desperate illness, we would mobilize ourselves to act immediately, to save ourselves. But since wilding is a societal disease and not a biological illness, individuals can feel a deceptive immunity. It is possible to feel healthy, have fun, and enjoy life as society begins to come undone.

But as the epidemic spreads, everyone will increasingly feel at risk. The personal meaning of the wilding epidemic is that we each have to spend more and more time simply defending our lives. Defending our property, defending our livelihood, defending our health, defending our physical safety, defending our ego. This imposes a terrible burden on the individual, and it can easily fuel the "me" mentality at the heart of the problem, but it also unlocks the riddle of what to do. Not only will the illusion of immunity diminish, but the wisdom of dealing with the underlying disease and not just the symptoms will become more apparent.

One can start defending one's life, as Albert Brook's film comedy of that title suggests, either wisely or foolishly. The shortsighted approach involves trying to save oneself by abandoning everyone else, exemplified by the suburbanites who cocoon within homes wired with the latest security technology and refuse to pay taxes to support the center city. Robert Reich suggests that such a "politics of secession" is sweeping upper middle-class America. If so, it is a blind and morally unsustainable choice, for it creates short-term symptomatic relief while worsening the disease.

Since the disease is social, so too must be the cure. As the social infrastructure begins to ulcerate and bleed, the rational long-term way to defend one's life is to help repair the damaged societal tissue, whether it be potholes in the road, hungry people sleeping on grates, or sociopathic competitiveness in the office. "Doing the right thing," then, is defending one's life by cooperating to build up community strength and bolster personal and collective resistance. This requires no saintly sacrifice for the common good, but tough-minded and clear-eyed assessment of where the threat lies. When facing a wilding threat, the first question to ask is, "What in myself or my social environment is creating this threat?" Once that question is answered, the next is, "What can I do about it?" Some cases will require purely personal change, falling back on all one's psychological and moral strength, as well as love and support from family, friends or mentors, to counter wilding impulses within oneself or susceptibility to wilding influence in the environment. Most cases will also require acting for some form of social change to extirpate the external poison, whether at work, in the neighborhood, or in the White House, typically achievable only with the help of others.

Fortunately, the wisdom of social action is obvious in a huge variety of circumstances, and Americans are already responding, especially where their own health is involved. When kids in Woburn, Massachussets, were getting sick because of toxic chemicals, parents got together to clean up the toxic dump and hold the wilding factory accountable. In the 1990s, Americans are recognizing that staying healthy has become a political-action project requiring a massive environmental clean-up, and they are not waiting for lackadaisical governments to take the lead. "People are recognizing they can in fact control their environment," Hal Hiemstra, a Washington environmental activist notes. "They're starting to say, 'we've had it.' " The *Boston Globe* reports that "an environmental wake-up call" is "being sounded nationwide by communities alarmed by the federal government's inertia and inspired by their own sense of power to reshape the landscape." The activists are not only defending their life but, the *Globe* observes, are "local heroes on planetary matters."[24]

Heroes of a different sort are the suburban communities around Minneapolis, who swam against the tide and rejected the "politics of secession," the suburban wilding that has helped push Bridgeport, Connecticut, into Chapter Eleven bankruptcy and left New York City and hundreds of other cities tottering on the brink. The Minnesota suburbs joined with Minneapolis in the mid-1980s and formed a regional pact "whereby any community enjoying 40 percent more than the average growth of the region in any given year would have to share with the other signers of the pact." Such apparent sacrifice for the larger good is just plain common sense, since if the city center failed, it would bring the surrounding communities down with it. The great irony, as John Shannon of the Urban Institute notes, "is that Minneapolis is now enjoying boom times and must pay *out* to the suburbs." A modern Aesop's fable, it shows how cooperation for the common good is, indeed, a form of enlightened self-interest.[25]

We can begin to cure the wilding sickness by doing more of what we have always done well and doing it better: taking responsibility for our lives through civic participation. Tocqueville was amazed at the richness of America's democracy; its dense web of voluntary associations and democratic town meetings made it unique. "The free institutions which the inhabitants of the United States possess, and the political rights of which they make so much use," Tocqueville explains, "remind every citizen, and in a thousand ways, that he lives in society." In other words, democracy, and more democracy, is the best antidote for wilding and the most nourishing food for the social infrastructure.

Americans have become apathetic and indifferent to national politics, but we still retain our propensity to join together in what Tocqueville called "an immense assemblage of associations." One researcher suggests that there are now over 500,000 self-help groups in the United States with over 15 million members; many, whether alcoholics, abused children, battered spouses, or "codependents," are casualties of the wilding epidemic who by joining with others are taking enlightened first steps toward not only recovering personally but rebuilding civil society. The same can be said of the millions of others involved in volunteer efforts or political activism at local or higher levels.

In a recent study, the Kettering Institute of Dayton, Ohio, concluded that Americans' indifference to national politics reflected less pure selfishness or apathy than despair about leaders and the absence of real choices. America desperately needs a new generation of political leaders who will tell the truth about the wilding crisis and articulate a new moral vision. But since no such leaders are now in view, the burden falls on the rest of us, where it ultimately belongs. It remains to be seen whether Americans will find in themselves the emotional and moral strength to forge a new collective dream.

Notes

Chapter One

1. "Move to Kill Victim Described by Defendant in Jogger Rape," *New York Times*, November 2, 1989, p. 1.

2. "Testimony Has Youths Joyous After Assault", *New York Times*, November 4, 1989, p. 1.

3. "Three Youths Jailed in Rape of Jogger," *Boston Globe*, September 12, 1990, p. 9.

4. "The Central Park Rape Sparks a War of Words," *Newsweek*, May 15, 1989, p. 40.

5. Quoted in the *Boston Globe*, January 11, 1990, p. 24.

6. Cited in article by Renee Graham, "Fur Store, Quiet Street are Now Macabre Meccas," *Boston Globe*, January 16, 1990, p. 20.

7. Colin Turnbull, *The Mountain People* (New York: Simon and Schuster, 1987).

8. Ibid. p. 86.

9. Ibid. p. 153.

10. Ibid. p. 132.

11. Ibid. p. 132.

12. Ibid. p. 137.

13. For an excellent book on the subject see: John Taylor, *Circus of Ambition: The Culture of Wealth and Power in the Eighties* (New York: Warner Books, 1989).

14. Donald Trump, *The Art of the Deal* (New York: Warner Books, 1987).

15. Taylor, *Circus of Ambition*, p. 8.

16. Laurence Shames, *The Hunger for More* (New York: Times Books, 1989).

17. Ibid. p. 27.

18. Ibid. p. 40.

19. Robert Reich, *The Work of Nations* (New York: Knopf, 1991).

20. I am indebted to Mike Miller for suggesting the terms "instrumental" and "expressive" wilding.

162   *Money, Murder, and the American Dream*

21. I am indebted to Mike Miller for his suggestion of "two Americas."

22. Kevin Phillips, *The Politics of Rich and Poor* (New York: Random House, 1990).

Chapter Two

1. *Los Angeles Times Book Review*, cited in Joe McGinniss, *Blind Faith* (New York: Signet, 1989).

2. Joe McGinniss, *Blind Faith*, p. 420.

3. Ibid. p. 62.

4. Ibid. p. 86.

5. Ibid. p. 89.

6. Ibid. p. 87.

7. Ibid. p. 308.

8. Ibid. p. 414.

9. Ibid. p. 297.

10. Ibid. p. 436.

11. Alison Bass, "Cold-blooded Killers Rarely Stand Out from the Crowd," *Boston Globe*, January 15, 1990, p. 34.

12. Ibid.

13. James Alan Fox and Jack Levin, "Inside the Mind of Charles Stuart," *Boston Magazine*, April 1990, pp. 66ff.

14. Alison Bass, "Cold Blooded Killers," p. 34.

15. Pete Hammill, "Murder on Mulholland," *Esquire*, June 1990, pp. 67–71,

16. Kathleen Hughes and David Jefferson, "Why Would Brothers Who Had Everything Murder Their Parents?" *Wall Street Journal*, March 20, 1990, p. A1. Joseph Poindexter, Robert Rand, J.D. Podolsky, "A Beverly Hills Paradise Lost," *People*, March 26, 1990, pp. 66–69.

17. "A Beverly Hills Paradise Lost," p. 66. *Time*, March 26, 1990, p. 24.

18. Hughes and Jefferson, "Why Would Brothers?" p. A10.

19. John Johnson, "Murdered Parents Led a Family of Competitors," *Los Angeles Times*. March 9, 1990, pp. 1, 29.

20. "A Beverly Hills Paradise," pp. 69, 72.

21. Hughes and Jefferson, "Why Would Brothers?" p. 1.

22. "A Beverly Hills Paradise," p. 69.

23. Ibid. p. 72. Hughes and Jefferson "Why Would Brothers?" p. 1.

24. "A Beverly Hills Paradise," p. 69.

25. Hughes and Jefferson "Why Would Brothers?" p. 1.

26. Lawrence Hussman, *Dreiser and His Fiction* (Philadelphia: University of Pennsylvania, 1983).

27. Ken Englade, *Deadly Lessons* (New York: St. Martin's Press, 1991).

NOTES 163

Chapter Three

1. George Gilder, *Wealth and Poverty* (New York: Basic Books, 1981), pp. 53–54.

2. Ibid. pp. 24–5.

3. Ibid. p. 25.

4. Ronald Reagan, cited in John Taylor, *Circus of Ambition*, p. 14.

5. Ronald Reagan, cited in Lewis Lapham, *Money and Class in America* (New York: Ballantine, 1988), p. 8.

6. Frank Sinatra and Barry Goldwater, cited in Paul Slansky, *The Clothes Have No Emperor* (New York: Simon and Schuster, 1989), p. 17.

7. Scott Burns, "Disaffected Workers Seek New Hope," *Dallas News*, August 21, 1988, p. Hi. Kevin Phillips, *The Politics of Rich and Poor* (New York: Random House, 1990), p. 165.

8. Noam Chomsky, personal communication, 1991.

9. Robert Reich, *The Resurgent Liberal and Other Unfashionable Prophecies* (New York: Random House, 1988), p. 8.

10. Cited in Connie Bruck, *The Predators' Ball* (New York: Penguin, 1988), p. 84. The material that follows draws heavily on Bruck's extraordinary account.

11. Ibid. pp. 39, 57, 98.

12. Ibid. pp. 287, 245, 246.

13. G. Christian Anderson cited in Bruck, *Predators' Ball*, p. 246.

14. David Nyhan, "The Land of Milken Honey," *Boston Globe*, April 26, 1990, p. 15.

15. Robert Lenzer, "A Tearful Milken Admits Guilt," *Boston Globe*, April 25, 1990, pp. 1, 25.

16. Bruck, *Predators' Ball*, p. 360.

17. Ibid. pp. 301, 314, 357–8.

18. Ibid. pp. 370, 360–1.

19. Ibid. pp. 301, 340.

20. Ibid. pp. 247–8. Phillips, *Politics of Rich and Poor*, p. 211.

21. Ibid. pp. 246–7.

22. On Atkins, see Taylor, *Circus*, pp. 22–52. Boesky's quote is cited in Slansky, *The Clothes Have No Emperor*, p. 176. Slanky also provides the data on the Billionaire Boys' Club on p. 196.

23. Michael M. Thomas, "Greed," *New York Review of Books*, March 29, 1990, pp. 3–4.

24. Robert Reich, *The Next American Frontier* (New York: Times Books, 1983), p. 141.

25. Nancy Reagan and Michael Dukakis both cited in Slansky, *The Clothes Have No Emperor*, pp. 12, 246.

26. Ibid. p. 122.

27. Ibid. pp. 124, 223, 244, 200, 246.

28. Lewis Lapham, *Money and Class in America* (New York: Ballantine, 1988), p. 103. Slansky, *The Clothes Have No Emperor*, p. 82.

29. David Nyhan, " 'For Sale' Signs Always up in Capital," *Boston Globe*, May 6, 1990, p. A25.

30. Slansky, *The Clothes Have No Emperor*, pp. 61–63.

31. Ibid. pp. 66, 110, 52, 38, 63.

32. Ibid. pp. 155, 159, 223, 227.

Chapter Four

1. Kevin Phillips, *The Politics of Rich and Poor*, pp. xxi, 212.

2. Ibid. pp. 210ff.

3. Eamon Fingleton, "Highly Speculative," *The Atlantic*, Vol. 267, June 6, 1991, p. 22.

4. Phillips, *Politics of Rich and Poor*, pp. 216–17.

5. Stephen Pizzo, Mary Fricker, and Paul Muolo, *Inside Job* (New York: McGraw-Hill, 1989), pp. 7–8. Citations from Seidman and Sessions in Thomas Hayes, "Sick Savings Units Riddled by Fraud, FBI Head Asserts," *New York Times*, April 12, 1990, p. 1.

6. "Deregulation Helped Turn S and L Problem into Crisis," *Miami Herald*, February 19, 1989. "S and L Failure: Stumbling on New Playing Field," *Boston Globe*, July 15, 1990, p. 10.

7. Larry Tye, "Neil Bush's S and L Woes May Return to Haunt His Father," *Boston Globe*, July 8, 1990, p. 21.

8. Stephen Kurkjian, "Bank Official Pushed Thrifts Sale," *Boston Globe*, July 10, 1990, pp. 1, 12.

9. Richard Behar, "Catch Us If You Can," *Time*, March 26, 1990, p. 60. Senator Metzenbaum cited in Stephen Kurkjian, "Bank Official Pushed Thrifts Sale." William Greider, "The Great S and L Clearance," *American Prospect*, Summer 1990, pp. 11–13.

10. William Greider, "The Next Bank Robbery," *New York Times*, May 29, 1991, p. A21.

11. Michael Quint and John C. Freed, "Bank Losses Worst in 50 Years, But No Danger to System is Seen," *New York Times*, February 17, 1991, p. 1.

12. Robert A. Rosenblatt, "Shaky Banks Could Create Second Nightmare," *Los Angeles Times*, September 17, 1990, pp. A1, A12.

13. William Greider, "Next Bank Robbery."

14. Ibid.

15. Ibid.

16. Dean Baquet, "Bureaucratic Snags Blocked BCCI Inquiry in '88," *New York Times*, August 13, 1991, p. A11.

17. Richard W. Stevenson, "Worry for an Industry Selling Peace of Mind," *New York Times*, May 12, 1991, p. 5.

18. Michael Lev, "California Backs $3 Billion Bid from French for Seized Insurer," *New York Times*, August 8, 1991, pp. A1, D5.

19. Ibid.

20. Jonathan Marshall, Peter Scott, and Jane Hunter, *The Iran-Contra Connection* (Boston: South End Press, 1987), p. 28.

21. Gary Sick, "The Election Story of the Decade," *New York Times*, April 15, 1991, p. A17.

22. Ibid.

23. Joel Bleifuss, "The First Stone," *In These Times*, May 15–21, 1991, pp. 4–5.

24. "Reagan's Hostage-Deal Hints," *Boston Globe*, June 19, 1991, p. 18.

25. Sick, "Election Story."

26. Elizabeth Drew, *Election Journal* (New York: Morrow and Co., 1989), p. 323.

27. Bob Woodward, *The Commanders* (New York: Simon and Schuster, 1991). See John B. Judis, "Why We Went to War," *In These Times*, May 15–21, 1991.

28. This harsh analogy is not intended, I stress again, to refer to the president's personal qualities, but his policies. As noted in Chapter 7, it is possible to be entirely decent in personal life and implement wilding practices in public life.

29. Noam Chomsky, "What We Say Goes: The Middle East in the New World Order," *Z Magazine*, May 1991, p. 51.

30. Ibid. Thomas Friedman, *New York Times*, August 22, 1990.

31. "U.S. Faced the Decision on War," *Boston Globe*, May 5, 1991, pp. 1, 24. Bob Woodward, *The Commanders*.

32. Cited in "Now, a Responsibility to Iraq," *Boston Globe*, May 27, 1991, p. 10. See also Walter V. Robinson, "Devastation Reigns in Iraq," *Boston Globe*, March 24, 1991, p. 1. Patrick E. Tyler, "Health Study Says Child Mortality Rate in Iraq Has Tripled," *New York Times*, October 22, 1991, p. A6.

33. Patrick E. Tyler, "U.S. Officials Believe Iraq Will Take Years to Rebuild," *New York Times*, June 3, 1991, pp. A1, A8.

34. Holly Sklar, "Brave New World Order," *Z Magazine*, May, 1991, p. 30.

35. AP, "Group Says up to 200,000 Died in Gulf," *Boston Globe*, May 30, 1991, p. 17.

36. Ibid. pp. 30, 31.

37. Steve Col and William Branigin, "U.S. Road Raid: Were Iraqis Needlessly Slaughtered?" *Washington Post*, reprinted in *Boston Globe*, March 14, 1991, p. 12.

38. Zbigniew Brzezinski, "Three R's for the Middle East," *New York Times*, April 21, 1991, p. 17. Anthony Lewis, "Politics and Decency," *New York Times*, April 15, 1991, p. A17.

39. Edward A. Gargan, "At Kuwaiti Trials, T-Shirt Gets Man 15 Years," *New York Times*, May 19, 1991, p. 1.

40. Nikolai Shmelyov, "The Rebirth of Common Sense," in Stephen F. Cohen and Katrina Vanden Heuvel, *Voices of Glasnost: Gorbachev's Reformers Speak* (New York: W.W. Norton, 1989), p. 151. "Lenin's City of Revolution is Now Nostalgic for Peter the Great," *New York Times*, June 24, 1990, pp. 1, A8.

Chapter Five

1. Jerry Thomas and Peter Canellos, "3 shot to death in Hub," *Boston Globe*, March 14, 1990, p. 1. Sean Murphy, "Driver Shoots BU Student After Prank." February 20, 1990, p. 1.

2. Susan Trausch, "The Generous Greed Machine," *Boston Globe*, March 14, 1990.

3. Rob Polner, "A Real Education in the New York City School System," *In These Times*, April 11-17, 1990, p. 12.

4. Taylor, *Circus of Ambition*, pp. 165-6. I owe much of the following discussion of Hollywood to John Taylor's work.

5. Ibid. p. 164.

6. Ibid. pp. 138ff.

7. Ibid. pp. 138-45.

8. Stuart Ewen, *All Consuming Images* (New York: Basic Books, 1988).

9. Charles Champlin, *Los Angeles Times*, cited in Taylor, *Circus of Ambition*, p. 149.

10. Stephen Pfohl, "Welcome to the Parasite Cafe: Postmodernity as a Social Problem" (mimeo, Boston College, 1990), pp. 11, 27.

11. Laurence Shames, *More*, pp. 147, 151, 153.

12. "Warning: The Standard of Living is Slipping," *Business Week*, April 20, 1987, p. 48.

13. Ibid, p. 66. Carolyn Shaw Bell, "Costs of the Mideast Crisis," *Boston Globe*. August 14, 1990, p. 24. Reich, *Resurgent Liberal*, p. 61. Robert Reich, *Next American Frontier*, p. 3.

14. "Warning: The Standard of Living," *Business Week*, p. 46.

15. Phillips, *Politics of the Rich and Poor*, p. 10.

16. "Warning," *Business Week*, pp. 46, 52. "The Face of the Recession," *Boston Globe*, August 14, 1990, pp. 24-5.

17. Donald Kanter and Philip Mirvis, *The Cynical Americans* (San Francisco: Jossey-Bass, 1989), p. 34.

18. Ibid. pp. 9, 10, 291,

19. Ibid. pp. 27-34.

20. Ibid. pp. 35-40.

21. Kanter cited in Charles A. Radin, "At Core, Say Analysts, U.S. Suffers Crisis of Confidence," *Boston Globe*, July 2, 1990, pp. 1, 5.

22. Kanter and Mirvis, *Cynical Americans*, pp. 10, 291.

23. Edward B. Fiske, "Fabric of Campus Life Is in Tatters, a Study Says," *New York Times*, April 30, 1990, A15.

24. Ibid.

25. Fox Butterfield, "Scandal Over Cheating at M.I.T. Stirs Debate on Limits of Teamwork," *New York Times*, May 22, 1991, p. 12.

26. William Celis 3d, "Blame to Share in Overcharging of U.S. for Research," *New York Times*, May, 12, 1991.

27. Elizabeth Kastor, "Magazine Boom: Mass Appeal to Yuppie Kids," *Boston Globe*, August 16, 1990, p. 85.

28. Gordon McKibbon, "It's in the (Baseball) Cards," *Boston Globe*, April 11, 1990, pp. 1, 12.

29. Michael Oreskes, "Profile of Today's Youth: They Couldn't Care Less," *New York Times*, June 28, 1990, p. D21.

30. Philippe Bourgois, "Just Another Night on Crack Street," *New York Times Sunday Magazine*, November 12, 1989, pp. 53ff.

31. Ibid. p. 62.

32. Ibid. p. 64.

33. Ibid. p. 62.

34. Ibid. p. 65.

35. Ibid. p. 94.

36. Ibid. p. 94.

Chapter Six

1. Craig Wolf, "Ten Teen-Age Girls Held in Upper Broadway Pinprick Attacks," *New York Times*, November 4, 1989, p. 27.

2. "Fears Rise of a City Consumed by Violence," *Boston Globe*, March 15, 1990, p. 12.

3. Ibid.

4. Ibid. Sally Jacobs, "As Streets Turn Deadly, Youths Revise Their Survival Code," *Boston Globe*, February 24, 1990, p. 1.

5. "Gang Violence Afflicts Cities Nationwide," *Boston Globe*, March 26, 1990, p. 10. Sam Roberts, "No, This City Is Not the One He Helped Save," *New York Times*, April 12, 1990, B1. "Booby Trap Death Brings Fine," *New York Times*, August 22, 1990.

6. Dirk Johnson, "In U.S. Parks, Some Seek Retreat, But Find Crime," *New York Times*, August 21, 1990, pp. 1, A20.

7. Ibid.

8. Ibid.

9. Richard J. Gelles and Murray A. Straus, *Intimate Violence* (New York: Simon and Schuster, 1988), p. 18.

10. Peter S. Canellos, "Killings by Young Believed on Rise," *Boston Globe*,

August 13, 1990, pp. 1, 18. "Boston Tries to Stem Tide of Violence Among Young People," *Boston Globe*, February 25, 1990, p. 31.

11. "Record U.S. Murder Rate Seen," *Boston Globe*, August 1, 1990, p. 1.

12. Turnbull, *Mountain People*, pp. 133–134, 136.

13. Chris Black, "The High Cost of a Gimme-Gimme Culture," *Boston Globe*, August 26, 1990, pp. A15–16.

14. Gelles and Straus, *Intimate Violence*, p. 18.

15. "Poll: 1 in 4 Jailed Killers Was Friend, Kin of Victim," *Boston Globe*, July 30, 1990, p. 5. William Stacey and Anson Shupe, *The Family Secret* (Boston: Beacon Press, 1983), pp. 2–3, 31, 66. Ethan Bronner, "For Youths, Family More a Threat than Strangers," *Boston Globe*, May 3, 1990, p. 1. Robert A. Rosenblatt, "Abuse of the Elderly, Most Often in Family, is Soaring, Panel Says," *Boston Globe*, May 1, 1990, p. 10.

16. Lloyd de Mause, ed., *The History of Childhood* (New York: Psychohistory Press, 1974).

17. Patrick Moynihan, "Toward a Post-Industrial Social Policy," *The Public Interest*, Fall, 1989, Lawrence Stone, "The Road to Polygamy," *New York Review of Books*, March 2, 1989, p. 14.

18. James R. Wetzel, "American Families: 75 Years of Change," *Monthly Labor Review*, March 1990, pp. 4–5, 9. Desiree French, "Second Marriages," *Boston Globe*, September 19, 1989, pp. 61–2. Stone, "The Road to Polygamy," pp. 12–15.

19. Wetzel, p. 9. Thomas Exter, "Look Ma, No Spouse," *American Demographics*, March, 1990, p. 83. See also Constance Sorrentino, "The Changing Family in International Perspective," *Monthly Labor Review*, March, 1990, p. 50.

20. Wetzel, "American Families," p. 11.

21. Ibid. Associated Press, "Over a Quarter of Babies Were Born to Unwed Mothers in '88, Study Finds," *Boston Globe*, June 14, 1991, p. 6.

22. Sorrentino, "The Changing Family," op.cit., pp. 46–7.

23. Stone, "Road to Polygamy," p. 15.

24. Edward Ginsburg, cited in Barbara Carton, "Divorce: What the Judge Sees," *Boston Globe*, May 22, 1991, pp. 79, 81.

25. L. J. Weitzman, *The Divorce Revolution* (Glencoe, Ill.: Free Press, 1985). Stone, "Road to Polygamy," p. 14. Jerrold Footlick, "What Happened to the Family?" *Newsweek* Special Issue on the Family, 1989, p. 16.

26. Barbara Kantrowitz and Pat Wingert, "Step by Step," *Newsweek* Special Issue, pp. 24, 27, 34.

27. Jonathan Kozol, "The New Untouchables," *Newsweek* Special Issue, p. 52.

28. Kenneth L. Woodward, "Young Beyond Their Years, *Newsweek* Special Issue, p. 57.

29. Dr. Benjamin Spock, "It's All Up to Us," *Newsweek* Special Issue, p. 106.

30. Tom Ashbrook, "A View From the East," *Boston Globe Sunday Magazine,* February 19, 1989, p. 16.

31. Ibid. p. 71.

32. Ibid. pp. 71-2.

33. Ibid. p. 76.

34. Philip Mitchell, "Saving State Roads," *Boston Globe*, March, 1990, p. 11. "Aging Roads, Bridges, Get Scant Notice," *Boston Globe*, April 11, 1990, p. 20.

35. Michael Albert, "At the Breaking Point?" *Z Magazine*, May, 1990, p. 17. Susan DeMarco and Jim Hightower, "You've Got To Spread It Around," *Mother Jones*. May, 1988, p. 36. Irene Sege, "Poverty, Disease, Poor Education Imperial Nation's Youth, Panel Says," *Boston Globe*, April 27, 1990, p. 6.

36. "Consensus Fuels Ascent of Europe," *Boston Globe*, May 13, 1990, p. 19.

37. Dolores Kong, "Mass. Cut May Slow Ambulance Response," *Boston Globe*, January 29, 1990, p. 1. "Many See Grim Side of Dukakis Budget; More Deaths, Illness, Poverty," *Boston Globe*, January 28, 1990, p. 28. Renee Loth, "Women and Children Last," *Boston Globe Sunday Magazine*, March 11, 1990, p. 17.

38. David Nyhan, "Tax-Package Turmoil," *Boston Globe*, July 17, 1990, p. 13.

39. Robert Kuttner, *Revolt of the Haves* (New York: Simon and Schuster, 1980), p. 10.

40. John Powers, "Whatever Happened to the Common Good?" *Boston Globe Sunday Magazine,* April 1, 1990, pp. 16-7, 38-42.

41. Suzanne Gordon, "Our Town Crumbles as Residents Idly Sit By," *Boston Globe*, February 24, 1990, pp. A1, A22.

42. These interviews were skillfully carried out by Boston College graduate students David Croteau and Mary Murphy.

Chapter Seven

1. Alan Wolfe, *Whose Keeper? Social Science and Moral Obligation* (Berkeley: University of California Press, 1989).

2. Alexis de Tocqueville, *Democracy in America*, Vol. II, (Cambridge: Sever and Francis, 1863), pp. 119-20, 121, 123.

3. Ibid. p. 128.

4. Ibid. p. 129.

5. Constance L. Hays, "Fall Kills Woman Trying to Help a Friend's Child," *New York Times*, May 15, 1991, p. B3.

6. Robert Preer, "Volunteers Plug Cash Gap in the Suburbs," *Boston Globe*, June 9, 1991, p. 1, 8.

7. Kathleen Teltsch, "Nowadays, Robin Hood Gets the Rich to Give to the Poor," *New York Times*, June 3, 1991, p. B1.

8. Virginia Ann Hodgkinson and Murray S. Weitzman, *Dimensions of the Independent Sector* (Washington D.C.: Independent Sector, 1989), pp. 7-9.

9. James Combs, *Polpop: Politics and Popular Culture in America* (Bowling Green: Green University Popular Press, 1984), p. 29.

10. Ibid. p. 34.

11. Phillips, *Politics of Rich and Poor.* Chapter 1.

12. James Reston, "A Persistent American Yearning," *New York Times Magazine*, June 16, 1991, p. 45.

13. Michio Morishima, *Why Has Japan Succeeded?* (Cambridge: Cambridge University Press, 1982), p. 3.

14. Amitai Etzioni, *An Immodest Agenda* (New York: McGraw-Hill, 1983), p. 94.

15. See Alan Wolfe, *Whose Keeper?* pp. 31ff. for an excellent discussion of the structural incompatibilities between the "free market" and civil society.

16. "Consensus Fuels Ascent of Europe," *Boston Globe*, May 13, 1990, p. 19.

17. Ibid.

18. Severyn Bruyn, *A Future for the American Economy* (Stanford: Stanford University Press, 1991). See also Bruyn, *The Field of Social Investment* (Cambridge: Cambridge University Press, 1987), and Bruyn and James Meehan, *Beyond the Market and the State* (Philadelphia: Temple University Press, 1985). See also Ritchie Lowry, *Good Money* (New York: W.W. Norton, 1991).

19. Bruyn, *Future for the American Economy.*

20. Lowry, *Good Money.*

21. John Kenneth Galbraith, "Let's Borrow More Money," *New York Times*, May 16, 1991, p. A23. Nicholas Leamann, "Healing the Ghettos," *The Atlantic*, March, 1991, p. 22. Holly Sklar, "These Kids Have Not Grown Up," *The Plain Dealer*, May 18, 1991.

22. For a review of health care proposals, see *The American Prospect*, Summer, 1991.

23. Paul Savoy, "Time for a Second Bill of Rights," *The Nation*, June 17, 1991, p. 815–16.

24. Larry Tye, "Local Heroes on Planetary Matters," *Boston Globe*, June 22, 1991, p. 3.

25. Renee Loth, "Small Cities, Big Problems," *Boston Globe*, June 23, 1991, pp. A25, A28.